MARY
BAKER EDDY

SPIRITUAL LEADERS AND THINKERS

MARY BAKER EDDY

MOHANDAS GANDHI

AYATOLLAH RUHOLLAH KHOMEINI

MARTIN LUTHER

AIMEE SEMPLE McPHERSON

THOMAS MERTON

DALAI LAMA (TENZIN GYATSO)

SPIRITUAL
LEADERS AND
THINKERS

MARY
BAKER EDDY

Rachel A. Koestler-Grack

Introductory Essay by
Martin E. Marty, Professor Emeritus
University of Chicago Divinity School

CHELSEA HOUSE
PUBLISHERS
A Haights Cross Communications Company
Philadelphia

CHELSEA HOUSE PUBLISHERS

VP, NEW PRODUCT DEVELOPMENT Sally Cheney
DIRECTOR OF PRODUCTION Kim Shinners
CREATIVE MANAGER Takeshi Takahashi
MANUFACTURING MANAGER Diann Grasse

Staff for MARY BAKER EDDY

EXECUTIVE EDITOR Lee Marcott
SENIOR EDITOR Tara Koellhoffer
PRODUCTION EDITOR Megan Emery
ASSISTANT PHOTO EDITOR Noelle Nardone
SERIES AND COVER DESIGNER Keith Trego
LAYOUT 21st Century Publishing and Communications, Inc.

www.chelseahouse.com

First Printing

9 8 7 6 5 4 3 2 1

Library of Congress Cataloging-in-Publication Data applied for.

ISBN 0-7910-7866-3

CONTENTS

Foreword

W hy become acquainted with notable people when making efforts to understand the religions of the world?

Most of the faith communities number hundreds of millions of people. What can attention paid to one tell about more, if not most, to say nothing of *all*, their adherents? Here is why:

The people in this series are exemplars. If you permit me to take a little detour through medieval dictionaries, their role will become clear.

In medieval lexicons, the word *exemplum* regularly showed up with a peculiar definition. No one needs to know Latin to see that it relates to "example" and "exemplary." But back then, *exemplum* could mean something very special.

That "ex-" at the beginning of such words signals "taking out" or "cutting out" something or other. Think of to "excise" something, which is to snip it out. So, in the more interesting dictionaries, an *exemplum* was referred to as "a clearing in the woods," something cut out of the forests.

These religious figures are *exempla*, figurative clearings in the woods of life. These clearings and these people perform three functions:

First, they define. You can be lost in the darkness, walking under the leafy canopy, above the undergrowth, plotless in the pathless forest. Then you come to a clearing. It defines with a sharp line: there, the woods end; here, the open space begins.

Great religious figures are often stumblers in the dark woods.

We see them emerging in the bright light of the clearing, blinking, admitting that they had often been lost in the mysteries of existence, tangled up with the questions that plague us all, wandering without definition. Then they discover the clearing, and, having done so, they point our way to it. We then learn more of who we are and where we are. Then we can set our own direction.

Second, the *exemplum*, the clearing in the woods of life, makes possible a brighter vision. Great religious pioneers in every case experience illumination and then they reflect their light into the hearts and minds of others. In Buddhism, a key word is *enlightenment*. In the Bible, "the people who walked in darkness have seen a great light." They see it because their prophets or savior brought them to the sun in the clearing.

Finally, when you picture a clearing in the woods, an *exemplum*, you are likely to see it as a place of cultivation. Whether in the Black Forest of Germany, on the American frontier, or in the rain forests of Brazil, the clearing is the place where, with light and civilization, residents can cultivate, can produce culture. As an American moviegoer, my mind's eye remembers cinematic scenes of frontier days and places that pioneers hacked out of the woods. There, they removed stones, planted, built a cabin, made love and produced families, smoked their meat, hung out laundered clothes, and read books. All that can happen in clearings.

In the case of these religious figures, planting and cultivating and harvesting are tasks in which they set an example and then inspire or ask us to follow. Most of us would not have the faintest idea how to find or be found by God, to nurture the Holy Spirit, to create a philosophy of life without guidance. It is not likely that most of us would be satisfied with our search if we only consulted books of dogma or philosophy, though such may come to have their place in the clearing.

Philosopher Søren Kierkegaard properly pointed out that you cannot learn to swim by being suspended from the ceiling on a belt and reading a "How To" book on swimming. You learn because a parent or an instructor plunges you into water, supports you when necessary, teaches you breathing and motion, and then releases you to swim on your own.

Kierkegaard was not criticizing the use of books. I certainly have nothing against books. If I did, I would not be commending this series to you, as I am doing here. For guidance and courage in the spiritual quest, or—and this is by no means unimportant!—in intellectual pursuits, involving efforts to understand the paths others have taken, there seems to be no better way than to follow a fellow mortal, but a man or woman of genius, depth, and daring. We "see" them through books like these.

Exemplars come in very different styles and forms. They bring differing kinds of illumination, and then suggest or describe diverse patterns of action to those who join them. In the case of the present series, it is possible for someone to repudiate or disagree with *all* the religious leaders in this series. It is possible also to be nonreligious and antireligious and therefore to disregard the truth claims of all of them. It is more difficult, however, to ignore them. Atheists, agnostics, adherents, believers, and fanatics alike live in cultures that are different for the presence of these people. "Leaders and thinkers" they may be, but most of us do best to appraise their thought in the context of the lives they lead or have led.

If it is possible to reject them all, it is impossible to affirm everything that all of them were about. They disagree with each other, often in basic ways. Sometimes they develop their positions and ways of thinking by separating themselves from all the others. If they met each other, they would likely judge each other cruelly. Yet the lives of each and all of them make a contribution to the intellectual and spiritual quests of those who go in ways other than theirs. There are tens of thousands of religions in the world, and millions of faith communities. Every one of them has been shaped by founders and interpreters, agents of change and prophets of doom or promise. It may seem arbitrary to walk down a bookshelf and let a finger fall on one or another, almost accidentally. This series may certainly look arbitrary in this way. Why precisely the choice of these exemplars?

In some cases, it is clear that the publishers have chosen someone who has a constituency. Many of the world's 54 million Lutherans may be curious about where they got their name, who the man Martin Luther was. Others are members of a community but choose isolation: The hermit monk Thomas Merton is typical. Still others are exiled and achieve their work far from the clearing in which they grew up; here the Dalai Lama is representative. Quite a number of the selected leaders had been made unwelcome, or felt unwelcome in the clearings, in their own childhoods and youth. This reality has almost always been the case with women like Mary Baker Eddy or Aimee Semple McPherson. Some are extremely controversial: Ayatollah Ruhollah Khomeini stands out. Yet to read of this life and thought as one can in this series will be illuminating in much of the world of conflict today.

Reading of religious leaders can be a defensive act: Study the lives of certain ones among them and you can ward off spiritual— and sometimes even militant—assaults by people who follow them. Reading and learning can be a personally positive act: Most of these figures led lives that we can indeed call exemplary. Such lives can throw light on communities of people who are in no way tempted to follow them. I am not likely to be drawn to the hermit life, will not give up my allegiance to medical doctors, or be successfully nonviolent. Yet Thomas Merton reaches me and many non-Catholics in our communities; Mary Baker Eddy reminds others that there are more ways than one to approach healing; Mohandas Gandhi stings the conscience of people in cultures like ours where resorting to violence is too frequent, too easy.

Finally, reading these lives tells something about how history is made by imperfect beings. None of these subjects is a god, though some of them claimed that they had special access to the divine, or that they were like windows that provided for illumination to that which is eternal. Most of their stories began with inauspicious childhoods. Sometimes they were victimized, by parents or by leaders of religions from which they later broke.

Some of them were unpleasant and abrasive. They could be ungracious toward those who were near them and impatient with laggards. If their lives were symbolic clearings, places for light, many of them also knew clouds and shadows and the fall of night. How they met the challenges of life and led others to face them is central to the plot of all of them.

I have often used a rather unexciting concept to describe what I look for in books: *interestingness.* The authors of these books, one might say, had it easy, because the characters they treat are themselves so interesting. But the authors also had to be interesting and responsible. If, as they wrote, they would have dulled the personalities of their bright characters, that would have been a flaw as marring as if they had treated their subjects without combining fairness and criticism, affection and distance. To my eye, and I hope in yours, they take us to spiritual and intellectual clearings that are so needed in our dark times.

Martin E. Marty
The University of Chicago

1

A Great Discovery

Mind is limitless.

—Mary Baker Eddy

On Thursday, February 1, 1866, Mary Baker Patterson walked down a snowy street in Lynn, Massachusetts. She and her friends exchanged pleasant conversation on their way to a Good Templars meeting. This social organization promoted alcoholic temperance, a popular cause at the time. Suddenly, Mary slipped on an icy patch of sidewalk and fell to the ground. Her head struck the ground violently, rendering her unconscious. Acting quickly, her friends carried her to a nearby house and sent word to Dr. Alvin Cushing, a well-respected homeopathic doctor and surgeon.

By the time the doctor arrived, Mary had awakened but was disoriented and unable to speak. She waved her arms and pointed to the back of her head and neck. Her wild actions indicated that she was in extreme pain. Upon examination, Dr. Cushing diagnosed Mary with a severe concussion and broken spine. At the very least, he suspected she would never take another step alone. Mary's friends agreed to stay the night and watch over her. During the night, Mary slipped into a coma. Her friends worried that her condition had worsened and she might die.

The next day, Dr. Cushing returned to check on Mary. She had regained consciousness and could speak well enough to demand to be taken home. The doctor advised her not to move, but Mary insisted. In order to lessen the pain, Cushing gave her a dose of strong medication, which plunged her back into a coma. Mary's friends wrapped her in fur robes and took her home by sleigh. A few hours later, Mary awakened. She remained bedridden all of Friday.

On Saturday, Dr. Cushing decided that there was nothing more he could do for Mary. He feared she was near death. All day long, friends hovered around her, and on Sunday, the minister paid a visit to prepare Mary for the worst. Mary refused to believe her health had failed her. When one of her friends was leaving the room, Mary confidently stated, "When you come down the next time, I will be sitting up in the next room. I am going to walk in."[1]

Shocked, her friend replied, "Mary, what on earth are you talking about?"[2]

That evening, Mary was alone with her Bible beside her. She turned to one of the healings of Jesus and began to read. She came to the passage "I am the way, the truth, and the life: no man cometh unto the Father, but by me" (John 14:6). As she read these words, Jesus flooded into her thoughts. She was filled with the conviction that God was the only life, and that her life was in God. She saw all things as spiritual, divine, and wholly good. In her thoughts, there was no room for pain, death, or fear. At that moment, her strength returned. She got up, dressed, and walked out of her bedroom unaided. Much to her friend's surprise, when she came back, Mary was indeed sitting up in the next room, just as she had predicted. A little while later, the minister came to call on Mary. When she met him at the door, he at first thought she was a ghost.

Everyone around her believed a miracle had occurred. The next day, Mary sent for Dr. Cushing, eager to show him how she had healed. He was both amazed and overjoyed at the sight of her. Shaking his head in disbelief, he asked Mary what had happened. Mary later wrote: "Even to the homoeopathic physician who attended me, and rejoiced in my recovery, I could not then explain the *modus* of my relief. I could only assure him that the divine Spirit had wrought the miracle."[3]

The experience changed Mary forever. She believed the incident was a divine revelation that she should devote her life to the newfound truth she had discovered. In later years, she declared, "That short experience included a glimpse of the great fact that I have since tried to make plain to others, namely, Life in and of Spirit; this Life being the sole reality of existence."[4] For three years, Mary withdrew from society to ponder her new calling and to search the Scriptures. She wanted to find the answers to what had made her well, which she believed was a divine state of mind.

Mary found her answers in the Bible, primarily in the healings of Christ. She focused on Jesus's method to miraculous cures, not questioning the afflicted about their disease or its symptoms. She contemplated the fact that Jesus neither prescribed drugs to support his divine power nor took them himself. Christ refused to drink a mixture of vinegar and gall (which incorporated poppy, from which the drug opium is derived) to lessen the pains of crucifixion. To Mary, these findings indicated that healing takes place in the mind. From her great discovery, she formed a religion of spiritual science and metaphysical healing—Christian Science. Mary dedicated the remainder of her life to teaching others this way of life. Today, many people still hold to her religious ideals.

2

Growing up

We are all sculptors, working at various forms,
moulding and chiseling thought.

—Mary Baker Eddy,
Science and Health with Key to the Scriptures

On July 16, 1821, a soft wind tickled the leaves on the apple tree outside the Baker homestead. The two-story saltbox farmhouse stood on a hill overlooking the Merrimack River valley. From the front yard, one could watch the golden fields of grain bend and bob in the breeze. The afternoon sun skipped across pastures of wildflowers and through orchards ripe with peaches, pears, and cherries.

Inside the modest house, Abigail Ambrose Baker gently rocked her newborn baby girl. Her husband, Mark, took only a short break from his farmwork to dote on his precious daughter. Mary Morse Baker was the last of six children. At the time of her birth, her brother Samuel had just turned thirteen, Albert was eleven, and George Sullivan was going on eight. Mary also had two sisters—Abigail was five years old and Martha was just a toddler.[5]

As the youngest child, Mary was especially cherished by her parents. But the special treatment she received did not seem to bother the other children, who also showered Mary with attention. Abigail later said of her sister, "I loved Mary best of all my brothers and sisters."[6]

Mark Baker owned five hundred acres of farmland in Bow, New Hampshire. He was an energetic man with a tough mind and a stern face. Mary later recalled, "My father possessed a strong intellect and an iron will."[7] Possessed of a powerful work ethic, Mark Baker rarely set aside time for leisure. He not only devoted long days to grueling farmwork, but he also spread himself throughout the community. Among his many roles, he held a position on the Bow town council, worked as a surveyor of roads, was a member of the school board, and served as chaplain to the local militia regiment. His drive did not end with assigned duties, however. When he saw a neighbor in need, he wasted no time in offering help, whether it was to shingle a house, chop wood, or plow a friend's field.

In contrast to her father's steely exterior, Mary's mother exhibited a soft kindness to all. The entire community viewed Abigail Baker as a woman of outstanding character. She had a

This is an artist's depiction (done around 1900) of the house in which Mary Baker Eddy was born in Bow, New Hampshire.

sympathetic heart, a light humor, and much common sense. One friend compared her to "the gentle dew and cheerful light."[8] Like many women of the era, Abigail Baker tirelessly performed her housework and lovingly raised her children without complaint, despite receiving little recognition for her efforts. Mary adored her mother. She later wrote: "Of my mother I cannot speak as I would, for memory recalls qualities to which the pen can never do justice."[9]

As a toddler, Mary grew close to her paternal grandmother, Mary Ann Moore. Mark, Mary's father, had inherited his land from his mother, and for this reason, she lived with the Bakers in their farmhouse. Mary Ann Moore spent long hours in her rocking chair with a Bible spread open on her lap. Little Mary would pull up her own tiny rocking chair next to her grandmother's, and the two of them would rock together. Mary quietly watched her grandmother study the Bible pages, sometimes pretending to read her own book.

PURITAN FAMILY

Mary was part of a strict Puritan family. Her father served as a clerk in the local Congregational church. Congregationalism was founded on the teachings of John Calvin, a sixteenth-century theologian whose ideas had a great impact on some Protestant religions of the time. John Calvin based his teachings on several principles—a belief in God as an omniscient, omnipowerful being, acknowledgment of the corrupt nature of all people, and the acceptance of a divine grace offered by God to a select group of people who will be saved from eternal damnation. This last principle was referred to as the doctrine of predestination; it was based on the notion that all human beings were condemned to spend eternity in hell, except for a small number whom God had chosen for salvation. Mark Baker firmly believed in predestination and openly expressed his beliefs when speaking to anyone about religion. Some nights, Mary would lie awake in her bed, listening to her father argue theological doctrine with friends and neighbors in the parlor. Mary later remembered forcing her eyes to stay open until the end of the discussion to find out who won the debate.

At a very early age, Mary learned that religion reigned supreme at the center of her family life. Every morning and evening, the family gathered for devotions and prayer. Her father read a chapter from the Bible, after which he launched into a lengthy sermon, during which, Mary said, Scripture passages "flowed from his lips in boundless measure."[10] Mary

OFF TO SCHOOL

The summer Mary turned five, she began to attend classes at a one-room schoolhouse a mile away from her home. It was the school her father had proposed and designed. Mary walked to school each day with her sisters and brothers. At recess, Martha and Abigail enjoyed showing off their little sister. Both children and adults were impressed by Mary's striking looks. Her dark hair curled softly around her pale cheeks, and her delicate frame moved with grace and confidence. Mary's blue-gray eyes stood out in contrast to her fair complexion, and when she became upset, they turned almost black.

One day in the schoolyard, Abigail set Mary up on a table and the schoolchildren gathered around. The older students began asking Mary questions. "What do you wish to be when you grow up?" Martha asked her. "When I grow up, I want to write a book!" Mary exclaimed. The other children laughed at Mary's response, knowing that most women of that time did not choose that type of profession. Most girls would have replied that they wanted to be a mother.[15]

But Mary had a natural zest for learning and intended to study hard to achieve her lofty goal. Unfortunately, she suffered from frequent bouts of illness as a child. Fevers left her bedridden for weeks at a time. It frustrated Mary to be absent from school for such long stretches. Mary's father believed her studies were making her sick. He often discouraged her from reading. The family doctor concurred with her father's suspicions and diagnosed: "She has got too much brains for her body; keep her out of doors, keep her in exercise, and keep her away from school all you can."[16]

Despite her father's warnings, Mary continued to work at her studies. She later admitted that schoolwork came easily for her, and, therefore, she did not have to study as hard as other children did. By age ten, Mary had mastered *Lindley Murray's Grammar* and the *Westminster Catechism*.

At home, Abigail Baker saw to it that the children were instructed in the Scriptures as well. Mary learned important moral lessons, such as "Love your neighbor as yourself" and "It is more blessed to give than to receive." While at school, Mary carried out these lessons quite literally. Mary sometimes gave her clothing away to needy schoolchildren. On winter days, it pained young Mary to see children shiver with cold. She generously forfeited her coat, scarf, or mittens for the sake of a poor friend. These occurrences became so frequent that when her mother dressed Mary for school in the morning, she urged, "My child, you must not give away your clothes today. Mother has not time to make others for you." [17]

At times, Mary's practical and "waste-not" nature got the better of her. On her way home from school one day, Mary noticed a pine log on the ground in her neighbor's woods. Mary liked the way pine logs blazed hot in the fireplace, and she imagined herself in front of the cozy fire, watching the orange flames leap up the chimney. Since the log seemed to be left for waste, Mary grabbed one end, and with some effort, managed to pull it home.

Abigail was not as excited to see the log as Mary was. She quickly asked Mary where she had found the log. "In Mr. Gault's woods," Mary replied. "Did you ask him for the log?" Abigail questioned. Mary promptly responded that she had not. "Carry it right back again, Mary, it is stealing for you to do that and God forbids you to steal," her mother instructed. Mary remembered how heavy the log was, and how hard it had been to drag it the whole way home. "Must I carry it back now I am so tired?" Mary asked. Abigail simply replied, "Would you have God and mother thinking till tomorrow that you have broken His commandment?" [18]

THE CALLING

Mary's interest in religion took a new turn when she was eight years old. From time to time, she began hearing a voice call her name—three times, each a little louder than the last. When she heard the voice, Mary immediately ran to her mother and asked what she wanted. Confused, Mrs. Baker replied, "Child, I did not call you."

"Mother, who *did* call me?" Mary asked. "I heard someone call *Mary*, three times!" As this same episode continued to repeat itself, Abigail Baker grew increasingly anxious. She wondered what was wrong with Mary and why she was hearing voices.

One day, Mary's cousin Mehitable visited the farm. While the two girls were playing together, Mary again heard the voice calling to her. This time, Mary pretended not to hear the voice and continued to play. Much to Mary's surprise, Mehitable looked at her in astonishment and sharply said, "Your mother is calling you. Why don't you go?"

Mary then hopped up from her spot on the floor and ran to her mother. But her mother had not called her. Once again, Mary explained how someone had called her name, but this time, her playmate had heard the voice as well.

Abigail was perplexed by this news. She asked to speak with Mehitable in private. Mary listened to their talk from the adjacent room. Abigail asked Mehitable if she had in fact heard a voice calling Mary's name. Mehitable answered positively that she had.

That night, when Abigail tucked Mary in, she read to her a story from the Bible about the prophet Samuel. In the passage, Samuel hears a voice calling to him and believes it is his teacher. When he asks the teacher what he wants, the teacher tells him he did not call. The teacher then instructs young Samuel to answer the voice, "Speak, Lord; for Thy servant heareth." The next time Mary heard the voice, she answered with these words. After that reply, she no longer heard the mysterious calls.[19]

A BATTLE WITHIN

Hearing what she believed was God's voice stirred Mary's heart and mind. The experience sparked a change in her view of the Lord and her father's religion. When Mary heard her name called, she immediately ran to her mother. The voice she heard was feminine, not masculine. She inwardly began questioning the Puritan religion and its doctrines. The more she contemplated God, the more she wondered if he truly was the stern and angry deity her father had portrayed—quick to punish the damned sinner.

Growing up, Mary's mother had taught the children to repent of their mischievous deeds. After punishment, the children responded by saying, "I am sorry and will not do so again." One day at age twelve, a troubled Mary came to her mother and asked her if eternal punishment really existed. Abigail gave Mary her full attention and answered, "Mary, I suppose it [does]."

"What if we repent," said Mary, "and tell God 'we are sorry and will not do so again'—will God punish us?" A moment of silence passed as her mother pondered these words. Mary continued, "Then He is not as good as my mother and He will find me a hard case." [20]

Another doctrine of the Congregational Church that Mary found troubling was the teaching of predestination. None of Mary's brother or sisters had been accepted into the church. Without acceptance, they were unable to be saved from eternal punishment. As Mary prepared for the day of her acceptance examination, she struggled with the realization that if she were admitted into the church, she would become a member of the elect. Mary later wrote: "I was unwilling to be saved, if my brothers and sisters were to be numbered among those who were doomed to perpetual banishment from God." [21]

Mary's very spirit was in conflict with the stern Calvinistic household to which she belonged. She had an insatiable hunger for learning and a true excitement for every breath of life. But the serious and solemn imposition of her religion threatened to stomp out her spirit at any moment. This inner battle frightened Mary. Her inner fears gave way to heated theological debates with her father. Her opposing views of religion caused an uproar in the Baker household. Arguments often escalated to an emotional outburst. At this point, Mary would collapse in an apparent fever. After these episodes, she remained bedridden for days.

It must have troubled Mary to cause so much anger and grief for her father, but the feelings inside her were strong and they only continued to grow stronger. The voice in her heart refused to be silent. Deep down, she knew she had to hold firm to her beliefs.

At age twelve, the day of Mary's examination drew near. Although she knew it was what her parents wanted, her mind was whirling with uncertainty. How could she profess to things she did not believe? Stricken ill by her thoughts, Mary took to her bed. As she burned with fever, her mother blotted her hot forehead with a cool cloth. She told Mary to lean on God for comfort and assurance. Mary closed her eyes and silently prayed to God for strength. As she prayed, Mary grew calmer. The anguish seemed to lift off her chest, and her fever came down. The doctor was amazed by Mary's sudden recovery. When Mary later recalled that moment, she wrote, "'the horrible decree' of predestination . . . forever lost its power over me."[22]

When the day of the examination arrived, Mary was present and ready. She answered the minister's questions with confidence. She then declared that she could not unite with the church if she had to accept its doctrine unconditionally: "I stoutly maintained that I was willing to trust God, and take my chance of spiritual safety with my brothers and sisters."[23] The minister was so moved by her heartfelt affirmation that he wept. After the examination was over, church members flooded to Mary and showered her with kisses for her moving speech. The clergy accepted her into the congregation, her protest along with her.

3

To Sanbornton Bridge

*To live and let live, without clamour for
distinction or recognition; . . . to write truth first
on the tablet of one's own heart—this is the sanity
and perfection of living, and my human ideal.*

—Mary Baker Eddy

I n January 1835, at age ninety-one, Mary's grandmother died. Although Mary Ann Moore had lived a full life, her death was hard on thirteen-year-old Mary. Mary treasured her childhood memories of her grandmother. At times, when she needed respite from the world, Mary returned to the soothing motion of her rocking chair—with the Bible resting on her lap.

After his mother's death, Mark Baker decided to sell the family farm in Bow and move to Sanbornton Bridge, a town about twenty miles north. He was excited over the prospects of new land, and Martha and Abigail were eager to enter the social ring of this booming industrial town. Mary did not share her family's enthusiasm, however. She felt strong ties to her childhood home, and the thought of moving away pulled tight strings around her heart. Not long after hearing the news, Mary fell ill, forcing her father to postpone the move until her health improved.

This delay probably relieved Mary for the time being. She did not stay ill forever, though, and in early 1836, the family made the twenty-two-mile trip to their new home. Before she left, Mary wrote a good-bye poem to her dear friend and neighbor, Andrew Gault. In it, she wrote,

> Hard is the task to take a final leave
> Of friends whom we shall see Ah! Never
> With unaccustomed grief my bosom heaves
> And burns with latent fire forever.[24]

Despite her initial protest, Mary quickly adjusted to life in bustling Sanbornton Bridge. Abigail and Martha enjoyed the social atmosphere, while Mary continued to concentrate on her schooling. Mary and Martha alternately attended Sanbornton Academy—a bare wooden building, without even a stove to heat it. The school had a room for girls and a separate room for boys, as was customary at the time. Mary's favorite subjects were natural philosophy, logic, and moral science.

Mary also found much comfort in poetry. Perhaps in writing she could escape the confines of her father's home. Although she enjoyed writing poetry, she apparently found it to be in conflict with her religious beliefs. When she was thirteen years old, Mary wrote:

> Above all our religion is as averse to all true poetry, as the most absolute atheism. No circumstance, perhaps, has exerted so powerful an influence in moulding [molding] the character, and directing the genius of the American people, as the peculiar nature of their religion. It contemplates man, not as much to live and enjoy life, but to prepare for an here- after. Hence whatever is thought, or said, or done, must be in reference to the tremendous issues of eternity. Such a religion is at war with the light, buoyant temper which delights itself in song.[25]

Despite the tug at her conscience, Mary continued to dabble in poetry, even publishing several of her works. She later wrote: "I thought that my mission was to write poetry, but my life has had more prose than poetry to it." [26]

Undoubtedly, Mark Baker could have afforded to send both of his daughters to school at the same time, but he was somewhat reluctant to pay for the tuition, perhaps seeing his daughters' education as frivolous. At times, brother George sent money for the girls' schooling. In April 1837, the school's writing master paid a visit to sixteen-year-old Mary, encouraging her to enroll in the next session. However, at the time, Mary was unable to attend. Her father simply would not provide the funds.

He also had strict rules for when suitors came to call on his beautiful daughters. When a young gentleman arrived at the door, Mark would greet him, "Let all conversation and pleasure be in harmony with the will of God." [27] He stood strongly against dances and forbade his daughters to attend them. However, like most teens caught up in youthful excitement, Martha and Mary managed to appear secretly at a few festive galas. Martha even succeeded in attending a Fourth of July ball. In a letter to George, older sister Abbie confided, "I suppose she would not have gone if she had asked consent; but she went without leave or license." [28]

Despite the shackles and chains her father placed on her, Mary blossomed into a lighthearted and cheerful young woman. Everyone who met her seemed to be captivated by her striking wide eyes and thick lashes, her flawless complexion, and her slim, graceful figure. Men often commented on her witty personality and her sunny disposition. One relative later wrote: "I've read of 'silvery' laughs lots of times, but her's [sic] came nearer to the realization of the novelistic description of anything in real life that I ever ran across." [29]

GENEROUS TEACHER

Along with her parents, Mary joined the Congregational church in Sanbornton Bridge. Inwardly, she still struggled with the doctrine of predestination, but it did not keep her out of the church. At age seventeen, Mary began teaching Sunday school to young children in the congregation. She loved children and, in turn, the students were drawn to her, too. They were particularly mesmerized by Mary's looks. One student recalled, "She [Mary] always wore clothes we admired. We liked her gloves and fine cambric handkerchief. She was, as I have come to understand, exquisite, and we loved her particularly for her daintiness, her high bred manners, her way of smiling at us." [30]

Mary's affection for children followed her out of the classroom. She took a special interest in Lyman Durgin, the Bakers' orphaned stable boy. The fact that the child did not attend Sunday school concerned Mary. One day, she questioned Lyman on the matter and discovered that he was too embarrassed to go to school because he could not read well. For this reason, he had trouble memorizing Bible verses and was unable to recite them with the other children.

It broke Mary's heart to see the poor boy so anguished by his weakness. She decided to tutor him. Each day, she read the Bible out loud to Lyman and instructed him to repeat her words. Soon, he was able to attend Sunday school and do recitations with the other students. Mary continued to be devoted to Lyman and tutored him for four years. Lyman probably received a more regular education than Mary ever did.

BELOVED ALBERT

Whatever learning Mary missed out on because of her father's stiff pocketbook, her brother Albert filled in. By the time the Bakers moved to Bow, Albert had already graduated from college. When he was home on vacation, Albert took it upon himself to educate his little sister. In fact, for one season, he taught his younger brothers and sisters at the village school. To Mary, Albert gave special attention—and private lessons. He taught Mary what she referred to as "smatterings" of Hebrew, Latin, Greek, and French.

Mary adored and admired Albert. She later described him, next to her mother, as "the very dearest of my kindred." She wrote in her autobiography, "To speak of his beautiful character as I cherish it, would require more space than this little book can afford."[31] Albert was a tall, impressive man, with a large head and chestnut hair. Mary later stated that he had a wonderful tenor voice, and people traveled from miles around to hear him sing. Albert proved to have great intellectual talent. Many people, including Mary, believed he was destined for success. For a few years, he read law in the office of future U.S. President Franklin Pierce. Albert was later admitted to the bar in both Massachusetts and New Hampshire, after which he returned to practice in the office Franklin Pierce had previously occupied. A short time later, Albert was elected to the New Hampshire legislature.

For Mary, Albert represented knowledge, culture, power, and intellectual success. Through her brother, Mary gained an early insight into the world of politics and law. He showed her a world more powerful, more educated, and more cultured than she had known under her father's roof. In addition to his intellectual strengths, Albert also exhibited a great deal of tenderness toward his family and friends. From Albert's character, Mary created a masculine ideal, and his memory later became a standard against which Mary compared all the other men in her life.

Albert's single flaw seemed to be his health, which caused a constant battle for survival. His frequent bouts with illness kept him from achieving his goals. In a letter to George, he wrote: "For several days I was almost entirely insensible, and think I must have died had they not carried me to the Hospital. I have now abandoned study forever, till my health is better."[32] For a while, Albert regained his strength and eventually won the Democratic Party's nomination for a congressional seat in 1841. But his health suddenly turned worse, and he died of kidney failure on October 21, before the election took place.

Mary was devastated by the death of her beloved Albert. Secretly, she vowed to succeed where Albert had failed and not to let her own fragile health keep her from achieving her goals. Looking for someone to lean on, Mary turned her affection toward her brother George. Albert's death must have seemed like the world's ending to Mary, but it was only a sliver of what was to come.

MARRIAGE AND TRAGEDY

Despite Mary's initial determination to live a full life, she soon let depression eat into her. A month after Albert's death, Mary wrote a poem that began, "O! health, for thee I languish."[33] In the poem, Mary revealed her fears of meeting an early death and being quickly forgotten. Even though she continued to be plagued with illness, she always managed to recover. And her cheerful nature promptly lifted her out of her dark moods.

During times of good health, Mary kept in close touch with her circle of friends. Among these were several male admirers— one of whom was her cousin, Hildreth Smith. The two friends spent countless hours discussing philosophy and reciting poetry. Before long, Hildreth fell deeply in love with Mary. However, he knew their relation to each other stood in the way of a marriage proposal. Unable to deal with his feelings, Hildreth moved to the South, where he later became a famous teacher and scholar.[34]

Mary turned her romantic attention to George Washington "Wash" Glover. Long ago, Glover had joked that Mary Baker would one day be his bride. The couple soon began corresponding through letters, and Glover may have begun to consider his earlier statement more seriously. After Glover moved to Charleston, South Carolina, he continued to keep in touch with Mary, even planning a summer visit to Sanbornton Bridge the summer she turned twenty. After his visit, the letters from Charleston came more frequently. Years later, Mary recalled, "In this way we got acquainted, for in writing to him I became very fond of him." [35]

Suddenly, without reason, Glover's letters stopped coming. Mary, of course, assumed the worst—perhaps he had met another woman. Heartbroken, Mary confided in her brother George, a close friend of Glover's. With George's help, Mary solved the mystery. Afraid of losing his youngest daughter to marriage, her father had intercepted the letters and withheld them from her. He could not bear the thought of Mary moving to faraway Charleston. He eventually gave Mary the hidden letters and agreed to the couple's marriage.

On Sunday, December 10, 1843, Mary and Glover were married in her father's parlor. Of Glover, Mary later wrote: "I married young the one I loved." [36] Following the wedding, the couple left for Concord, making a quick stop in Bow. They then traveled to Boston by train—still a fairly new mode of transportation. From there, they boarded a ship for South Carolina. During the voyage, the ship encountered stormy weather, and Mary became "hopelessly seasick." But her spirits lifted when for the first time her eyes gazed upon the wide, handsome streets of Charleston. She marveled at the beautiful magnolias in full bloom and the stately buildings that lined the streets.

After a one-month stay in Charleston, the newlyweds traveled to Wilmington, North Carolina, where Glover had business. In choosing a husband, Mary had certainly picked a successful one. Glover was outgoing, energetic, and business-minded. He had arrived in South Carolina in 1839, and within five years, he had established a prosperous building company. His latest venture was the construction of a cathedral in Haiti.

Mary gleamed in the limelight at social events where she met her husband's high-society acquaintances. One Wilmington resident described Mary as "a very beautiful woman, brilliant in conversation, and most gracious in her manner."[37] She gracefully stepped into the most distinguished literary circles. Mary contributed some of her writings to the Wilmington paper, including poems and reviews of theatrical performances. On one occasion, she was invited to write toasts for a Democratic Party dinner. Several of her pieces also appeared in a new publication called *Heriot's Magazine: The Floral Wreath & Ladies Monthly Magazine*. An advertisement in the Charleston newspaper described the magazine as containing "besides original contributions, a variety of selections in prose and verse from the most popular American female writers, and distinguished writers of this city."[38]

In June, tragedy brought an end to what had started as a Southern fairy tale. The building that stored all of Glover's materials for the Haitian cathedral, in which he had invested much of his money, was destroyed. Mary was six months pregnant at the time. In later years, Mary could not recall whether the materials were stolen or whether the building burned down. Mary's blurred recollection was probably due to the greater disaster that followed. Glover contracted a serious case of yellow fever and died on June 27, 1844. Soon to be a mother, Mary was left widowed and penniless. In a poem, Mary wrote: "I am now alone in soul."[39]

4

Years of Trial

What is left of earth to me!
—Mary Baker Eddy,
Retrospection and Introspection

With no family in the South, Mary made a long, sad journey north to Sanbornton Bridge. Her parents welcomed her back into their home. Mary found it difficult, however, to return to her old life after so much had changed.

On September 12, 1844, she gave birth to healthy baby boy. She named him George, Jr., in memory of her husband. Still exhausted from her recent trip, the delivery of George took a devastating toll on Mary's weak body. Unable to care for her newborn son, she sent George to a nursemaid who could take care of the baby until she regained her strength. Even after little George returned home, Mary had trouble tending to her motherly duties. Although there were days when she felt well, she just never seemed to recover fully from her illness. At times, she became so weak that she barely got out of bed. Her father worried about her delicate health. He sometimes picked her up in his arms and rocked her like a little child. Some days, he would have the street spread with straw to muffle the noise of passing wagon wheels so she would not be disturbed.

The Bakers' nurse, Mahala Sanborn, did most of the caring for Mary's son. Being physically unable to carry out the responsibilities of motherhood certainly tore at Mary's heart. All her life, she held a deep affection for children and desperately wanted to have children of her own. Her inability to care for George caused feelings of guilt and inadequacy. She later wrote: "The true mother never willingly neglects her children in their early and sacred hours, consigning them to the care of nurse or stranger."[40]

As Mary slowly regained her strength, she began to search for some type of employment to support herself and her son. Like many women of the time, Mary had few skills, and her social standing prohibited her from taking a job in the textile mills or factories. Social graces aside, the dirty conditions of nineteenth-century factories would have posed a tremendous risk to Mary's health. At last, she decided that her only recourse was to become a teacher. In 1846, with the help of her sister Abigail, Mary opened a small school for young children—equivalent to a modern kindergarten. Although Mary and her siblings had attended such a school in Bow during the summer, a school for youngsters was actually a fairly radical idea in New England.

In her school, Mary practiced innovative teaching methods, especially in the area of discipline. Instead of severely punishing students when they misbehaved, she rewarded them for good behavior. She later explained, "The way to have children stop doing wrong is to have them love to do right."[41] Mary's fresh approaches to teaching met with harsh criticism from the conservative parents of Sanbornton. To make matters worse, her health remained unstable, and George, Jr., continued to demand more time and energy from her. Eventually, her experimental school failed.

Twenty-six-year-old Mary again returned to writing, and, in between chasing little George around the house, she managed to compose numerous political articles for the Democratic paper *Hill's Patriot.* She also contributed to such publications as *Freemason's Weekly* and the *I.O.O.F. Covenant.* About this time, many people were packing their wagons and heading to the newly opened Western frontier. Confined by illness much of the time, Mary dreamed about taking the adventurous journey to a new land. Her daydreams inspired her to write a novelette entitled *Emma Clinton, A Tale of the Frontier.* However, she made little income from her writings and was left dependent on her family for support.

Although Mary was a widow with a son, her youth and beauty still drew the attention of Sanbornton's single men. One eligible young suitor was John Bartlett, a Harvard law student who began visiting Mary during his vacations from school. The many callers coming and going from the Baker home became the talk of the town. When Bartlett left for his last year at Harvard, Mary told a friend that at least now the neighbors would mind their own business about them, "as I am getting a little *mad* at their *lies,* for such they are."[42]

Eventually, though, romantic feelings did grow between Mary and Bartlett, because she traveled to Cambridge, Massachusetts, to attend his graduation in 1848. Shortly after, Mary made up her mind to marry the promising young lawyer. In 1849, however, news of gold being discovered in California delayed their plans. Along with thousands of other Americans, Bartlett caught "gold fever" and joined the migration west. The couple agreed to marry on his return or when Mary could join him in the West. It seemed to Mary as though her life were again on the road to happiness.

"WHAT IS LEFT OF EARTH TO *ME*!"

Mary's vision of a peaceful life with a family of her own quickly shattered. While Bartlett was away, her health deteriorated, and she was sent to Warner, New Hampshire, for two months to undergo treatment. Doctors believed she was suffering from a stomach ailment called dyspepsia. Shortly after Mary returned home, her mother, Abigail, passed away on November 21, 1849, at the age of sixty-five. Still grieving her mother's passing, only three weeks later, Mary received a letter from Sacramento, announcing Bartlett's death there. "What is left of earth to *me*!" Mary wrote in a letter to her brother George.[43]

Life in the Baker household continued to toss and turn. Mary suffered from recurrent illness, and her delicate health required Mahala Sanborn to spend an increasing amount of time in the Baker home. Then, in October 1850, Martha's husband died, and she moved back home with her two daughters. Mark Baker remarried in December to Elizabeth Patterson Duncan and decided he could not provide a home for his new wife, two widowed daughters, and three grandchildren. Martha went to live with her late husband's relatives, but her father still had Mary and little George on his hands.

Still mourning the loss of her mother, Mary was less than enthused about her father's quick remarriage. In a letter to George, she wrote: "Now he [Father] comes to me to help arrange the things of his bride; but I will see them in the bottomless pit before doing it. Everything of our departed Mother's has to give place to them and Father is as happy as a school boy."[44] Mary also felt some resentment toward her father for his cruel treatment of her son, George. She wrote: "In the spring he told me if George was not sent away he would send him to the *Poor House* (after abusing him as he did through the winter)."[45]

With no place to go, Mary went to stay with her sister Abigail, who graciously opened her home. However, much to Mary's horror, Abigail refused to let seven-year-old George stay with them. Abigail had a boy of her own about George's age, and the activity of two boisterous children was too much for her. As much as it pained Mary to send her son away, she had no other choice. Mary set up a temporary situation, sending George to live with Mahala—who had been like a second mother to him. Mary later recalled, "The night before my child was taken from me, I knelt by his side throughout the dark hours, hoping for a vision of relief from this trial."[46]

Before long, Mahala and her new husband, Russell Cheney, decided to move to the town of North Groton, forty miles away. Mary trusted that George was in good hands, but it hurt her desperately to let him go. She wrote about his leaving in a letter: "Oh! how I *miss him* already! There seems nothing left me now to enjoy."[47]

After George's departure, Mary's health took a quick decline. During the summer of 1852, she became so ill that her family feared she would not recover. In a letter to a friend, Martha wrote: "There is scarcely a ray of hope left us of her recovery. Her strength gradually fails, and all the powers of life seem yielding to the force of disease."[48] Over the years, Mary had tried many different treatments for her illnesses, including radical new medical fads such as mesmerism and homeopathy. Mesmerism was a treatment started by Switzerland's Dr. Franz Mesmer; it eventually gave way to modern hypnosis. Homeopathy is a system of therapy in which the patient is given a drug that would produce the same symptoms of the illness in a healthy individual. These types of treatment brought temporary relief to Mary's symptoms but never fully cured her. Mesmerism may have helped a little more than any drugs she was taking, as her illness was probably aggravated in part by the psychological grief of losing her son. For this reason, she was determined to get George back. Mary's only chance of bringing George home was either to find a way to support herself or get married.

DR. PATTERSON

Near the end of 1852, Mary was plagued by a toothache. She went to see Dr. Daniel Patterson, a relative of her father's new wife. Patterson was a tall, handsome, cheerful man, with dark hair and an unruly beard. He did not have the same intellectual flair as Mary, but she seemed to be drawn to his simple nature. After several professional visits, the two began corresponding on a personal level.

By March 1853, the two were engaged, but one issue threatened to stop the marriage—religion. Patterson was a Baptist. As was typical of the time, he expected Mary to convert to his religion. After much deliberation, Mary wrote him: "I have a fixed feeling that to yield my *religion* to yours I *could not*, other things compared to this, are but a grain to the universe."[49] Certain that this would be the end of their courtship, she concluded, "*Farewell.* May God bless and protect you."[50]

Patterson quickly responded to Mary's letter. He felt that it was completely within reason for him to ask such a conversion of her. Knowing that her father had influenced her decision, he wrote: "If your Father did counsel in that matter as you decided I wish simply that you would just ask him, who would have yealded [yielded] if there had been the same point of difference between him and his wife."[51] For a while, the couple postponed any plans for marriage, but Patterson still worked on Mary's teeth. Her visits gave him an opportunity to mend fences. By the end of April, the two had smoothed over their differences, and the engagement was back on.

In June, Mary and Patterson were married. Although Mary seemed to have sincere affection for Patterson, she later wrote in her autobiography: "My dominant thought in marrying again was to get back my child."[52] Unfortunately, her hopes did not go as planned. Patterson was reluctant to bring George into his home. He was concerned about Mary's unstable health, and to make matters worse, the couple began to undergo financial strains. Until they were secure, all hopes of regaining George were dashed.

Eventually, they borrowed money from Mary's sister Martha. In March 1855, the couple bought a house in North Groton. Finally near her son, Mary felt as though her wish had been granted. Initially, she hoped for frequent visits with George, but Patterson would not allow the two to see each other. George, now eleven years old, had grown up without much discipline. Patterson worried that the boy's rambunctious manner and apparent lack of schooling would upset Mary. His attempt to protect Mary from hurt backfired. Without Mary's knowledge, the Cheneys joined the migration west in April 1856, taking George with them. They planned to settle in Minnesota, which seemed like worlds away to Mary.

The news struck Mary a heavy blow, and she suddenly became deathly ill. Forced to devote endless hours to caring for his invalid wife, Patterson could not make enough money in isolated North Groton to support his household. He had to travel the countryside in search of work, leaving Mary in the care of a blind girl.

The couple's desperate state left them unable to pay Martha the interest on their loan. For the sake of her sister, Martha did not want to foreclose on the property, but her financial situation left no other choice. In March 1860, an auction was held and the house was sold. Patterson was gone at the time, and Mary was forced to leave the house alone. She moved to a rooming house in nearby Rumney. When Patterson returned, he managed to settle her in a house.

Amid the clouds of Mary's life, some light finally managed to break through in 1861. On October 10, she received a letter from George—the first communication in more than five years. The Civil War had broken out in April, and, consequently, seventeen-year-old George ran away from the Cheneys and enlisted in the Union Army. There, he met David Hall, a man who wrote letters for illiterate soldiers. Through Hall, George was able to track down his mother. The letter brought tears of joy to Mary's eyes. After this first contact, Mary received regular mail from George until he was wounded a year later. Still battling illness and often alone, Mary found much comfort in the letters from her long lost son.

Patterson, too, joined the Union cause, and in 1862, he traveled to Washington, D.C., on a mission for the governor of New Hampshire. While inspecting the battle lines near Bull Run, he was captured by Confederate soldiers. Upon hearing of her husband's imprisonment, Mary's health took a turn for the worse. Mary's sisters and brothers felt it was time to put more energy into finding a cure for her chronic ailments. During 1861, before Patterson traveled to the South, the couple had sent a letter to a Phineas P. Quimby in Portland, Maine. Quimby was reputed to have successfully cured numerous illnesses using his system of "mind cure." At the time, Quimby was unable to visit New Hampshire. While Patterson was away at war, Mary wrote to her sister Abigail, requesting money to visit Quimby's office in Maine.

Abigail was unconvinced of Quimby's cures and refused to pay for such a radical method of healing. Instead, she agreed to send Mary to Dr. W. T. Vail's Hydropathic Institute. Vail's treatment consisted of a water cure—drinking lots of water and taking baths. The method proved unsuccessful for Mary. One day, a former patient of Quimby's paid a visit to the institute and, after praising the great doctor's treatment, instilled new hope in Mary. She again wrote to Abigail insisting that she be allowed to meet with Quimby. This time, Abigail agreed to foot the bill. From Boston, Mary boarded a boat to Portland, not knowing how much her life was about to change.

5

The Cure

The time for thinkers has come.
Truth, independent of doctrines and time-
honored systems, knocks at the portal of humanity.

—Mary Baker Eddy,
Science and Health with Key to the Scriptures

Accoording to Quimby, all sickness is in the mind. He believed that illness and pain were brought on by sin. In order to be healthy, he professed, all a patient needed to do was replace his or her "wrong thinking" with pure thoughts. He taught his patients that within them existed a higher self, which he called "the mind of Christ." Once the patient achieved this state, true thoughts would fill the mind and ailments would disappear. "The truth," he declared, "is the cure."[53]

Quimby's practice grew from his interest in mesmerism. He discovered that he had a talent for hypnotizing people and soon found he could heal the sick through what would later be known as psychological therapy. Eventually, he came to believe that people had the power to both cause and cure their illnesses. He even used New Testament miracles performed by Jesus as an example of mind cure to support his theory.

When Mary arrived at the hotel in Portland, she had to be carried up the stairs to her room. The trip had been exhausting for her weak body, and she immediately took a rest. Later that day, she met Quimby in the hotel lobby. Thoroughly impressed by him, Mary wanted to begin treatment right away. As part of his treatment, Quimby wet his fingertips and placed them on Mary's head. He believed every human being was surrounded by a vapor that held his or her state of mind. By using water, he hoped to penetrate the mist around Mary. While he touched her, Quimby talked about her illness and encouraged her to purify her mind.

Initially, the cure seemed to work miracles for her. After only a week of visits, Mary was able to walk up 182 steps to the dome of the Portland city hall. In later years, Mary claimed that each time she entered Quimby's office she immediately felt better, so strong was her faith in his method. A month after her first visit, she sang his praises in a letter to the *Portland Evening Courier*. "As he speaks as never man before spake, and heals as never man healed since Christ, is he not identified with truth?" she wrote. "And is not this the Christ which is in him?"[54]

In September 1862, Patterson escaped from a Confederate prison and joined Mary in Portland. While in captivity, he had suffered terrible hunger and upon his escape he weighed only half what he had weighed before the war. Mary later recalled, "So changed by his suffering was he that his brothers did not know him."[55] Nonetheless, Mary was overjoyed and relieved by Patterson's safe return.

After a while, the couple decided to return to Sanbornton. Her family was surprised to finally see Mary in good health. In a letter to Quimby, she wrote: "I am to all who see me a living wonder, and a living monument of your power."[56] At the same time, Mary could not help feeling that Quimby's cure conflicted with her religious beliefs. She told a friend, "If all diseases are unreal and not good, God who is good and real should be our only healer, and I believe that if we only knew how to ask Him we should need no other."[57] Although Quimby professed that the key to healing is Christ-like thoughts, he did not call upon God in his practice. Quimby's son later wrote of his father's system: "There were no prayers, there was no asking assistance from God or any other divinity. He cured by his wisdom."[58]

Despite her initial optimism, as time away from Quimby stretched from weeks to months, Mary's condition again began to worsen. She returned to Portland in the middle of 1863. There, Mary spent day after day in Quimby's office—this time for more than just her own treatment. Wanting to learn more about his mysterious methods, she observed the treatments of other patients. She often spent long afternoons with Quimby, asking him questions and discussing his theories. Quimby was thrilled to share his ideas with Mary and called her a "devilish smart woman." At home, Mary stayed up late into the night, writing down her thoughts.

Although Mary's health remained stable, her life once again took some jarring blows. Her marriage slowly became strained. Patterson spent most of his time traveling and was gone for days at a time. When he was home, he found Mary's new enthusiasm for Quimby's cure annoying. He tired of her constant talk about mind healing and her Christian explanations of Quimby's theories. On the other hand, rumors about Patterson and his female patients abounded. Mary's troubles mounted when her father died in October 1865. Three months later, Quimby died of cancer. These events left Mary feeling incredibly alone and deserted. In a few weeks, however, Mary's life would take a surprising turn.

THE BEGINNINGS OF MORAL SCIENCE

Several weeks after Quimby's death, Mary underwent her near-fatal fall on the ice and her miraculous recovery. Her experience left her with many questions, and she spent late nights searching the Bible for answers. Personal affairs also continued to trouble her. Mary's husband had seemingly disappeared, leaving her unable to pay her rent of $1.50 per week. Eventually, she was evicted from her rooms and forced to stay with friends. In July, Patterson returned to Lynn, but quickly left again, this time eloping with one of his patients. Like Patterson, the woman was married. Upon finding his wife missing, her husband set off in pursuit of the couple. He caught up with them and brought his wife home. Mary could not overlook the situation and was granted a divorce.

Left without a steady income, forty-five-year-old Mary relied on her friends for support. She moved from home to home, staying as long as anyone would have her. She continued to pray and study the Bible for hours and wrote detailed commentaries on her findings. Her religious struggles and determination to uncover the science that governed healing annoyed her hosts, and was probably, in part, the cause of her frequent moves.

Abigail and her husband, Alexander Tilton, had become the most esteemed and prosperous citizens of Sanbornton, which would soon be renamed Tilton. Abigail offered to build a house for Mary next door to her own home. But Abigail stipulated, "There is only one thing I ask of you, Mary, that you give up these ideas which have lately occupied you, that you attend our church and give over your theory of divine healing."[59] Mary graciously declined the offer, replying she could not give up "this one thing I do."[60]

In autumn, Mary was invited to stay with the Ellises in Swampscott, Massachusetts. Fred Ellis was the village school-master, a pleasant young man, and his mother's heart went out in sympathy to Mary because she had endured so much. Mary spent all day writing in her room with what she later described as "fierce heart-beats." She was probably composing the first volume of her later work *The Bible in Its Spiritual Meaning*, titled *Genesis*. In the evening, she shared her work with the Ellises. Fred recalled, "She would read the pages to Mother and me, inviting, almost demanding, our criticisms and suggestions."[61]

As a starting point for her metaphysical studies, Mary went back to the beginning of all things: in "the beginning was God." Quimby had started his theories with animal matter. Mary, on the other hand, started with God, or Spirit. In her manuscript, Mary referred to Quimby's practices as "the twilight of discovery." Mary used his concepts, but built her own theories over and around them. When interpreting the creation account in *Genesis*, she paid special attention to the "evening" preceding the "morning" on the first day. According to Mary, this account had nothing to do with creation of the physical universe. Rather, it spoke of the step-by-step appearing of spiritual reality. Ideas stir in the shadows of human thought until the moment of revelation dawns—"the light of Truth." Later, Mary described evening as the "mistiness of mortal thought," and morning as "revelation and progress."[62]

In late autumn 1866, Mary moved to the Clark boarding-house on Summer Street in Lynn. The parting from the Ellises was a pleasant one, but for unknown reasons, she felt it was time to move on. She joined the thirteen other boarders each night for dinner, where she discussed her religious ideas. The innkeeper's son, George Clark, remembered that she "easily dominated attention when she cared to talk, and she was always listened to with interest. Every one liked her and admired her, though sometimes her statements would cause a protracted argument."[63]

Mary's ideas especially hooked the attention of young shoe-maker Hiram Crafts, who was also staying at the boardinghouse. She began to teach him about the healing, which at this time, she called Moral Science. At the end of his stay, Crafts asked Mary to return with him and his wife to their home in East Stoughton, Massachusetts. In return for room and board, she continued to instruct Crafts in her science of healing.

In spring 1867, Crafts abandoned his cobbling trade to become a healer. His family and Mary moved to the larger town of Taunton. On May 13, an advertisement appearing in the local newspaper read, "Dr. H. S. Crafts, would say unhesitatingly, *I can cure you.*" [64] The ad announced that Crafts had successfully treated illnesses such as consumption, dyspepsia, and rheumatism and also included a testimonial from a cured patient. Crafts's practice quickly grew, and in the evenings, Mary continued to advise him. The association with her first pupil did not last the year, however. Mrs. Crafts became increasingly annoyed by the amount of time her husband was spending with Mary. Not wanting to cause a disturbance in their marriage, Mary packed her bags and left.

THE GROWTH OF CHRISTIAN SCIENCE

With the help of friends, Mary found boarding at the house of "Mother" Webster in Amesbury, Massachusetts. Webster gave her a large sunny room and her own desk, where Mary contin-ued her writings. After a few months' stay, Mary decided to resume her teaching practices, only this time to a large audience. On July 4, 1868, she advertised in a Spiritualist paper for "any person desiring to heal the sick." She assured, "No medicine, electricity, physiology or hygiene required for unparalleled success in the most difficult cases. No pay required unless this skill is obtained." [65]

Before the lessons began, however, Webster's son returned home and insisted that Mary leave. She was sent out into the street on a rainy night. She found temporary housing down the street at the home of Sarah Bagley, where she lived throughout the summer. There, she met nineteen-year-old Richard Kennedy. Mary, Bagley, and Kennedy became fast friends, and Mary started instructing them in her newly discovered science. Before long, Mary was forced to leave because Bagley needed to find a boarder who could pay more rent. She moved to a place in Stoughton, but continued to teach Kennedy through the mail.

While in Stoughton, Mary completed her first version of a book on Moral Science, which she called by different names, including *The Science of the Soul* and *The Science of Man*. In her book, she illuminated the difference between Quimbyism and her own healing methods. According to Quimby, the human mind healed the disease. Mary, on the other hand, said "that God is the only healer and healing Principle, and that Principle is divine not human."[66] She found a publisher willing to print the book for a $600 fee. Unable to come up with the money, Mary returned to Bagley's again.

In late spring 1870, Mary's ambitions took an upward swing. She and Kennedy signed a three-year partnership agreement. Mary agreed to teach, and Kennedy would use her methods to heal. They moved to a small private school in Lynn and hung a sign announcing "DR. KENNEDY" from a tree branch outside the front door.

For Kennedy to set himself up as a doctor was not an unusual feat in the 1800s. Neither medical practices nor medicines were regulated, and newspapers were filled with columns advertising all sorts of newfangled treatments, such as mesmerism, magnetic treatment, and phrenology. In the beginning, Mary and Kennedy were one small practice competing with hundreds, but within a few short months, they became quite successful.

On July 15, Mary wrote a letter to Bagley announcing their great achievements. "I have all calling on me for instruction," she declared. "Richard is literally overrun with patients."[67] In August, Mary again advertised to teach classes in Moral Science, and this time she attracted six students. Each student agreed to pay a $100 fee for the instruction. She held evening classes for the following three weeks. As a textbook, Mary used copies of her manuscript, *The Science of Man.* Mary's enthusiasm inspired her students. One observer later wrote: "She was able to impart in her classroom: a feeling so strong that it was like the birth of a new understanding and seemed to open to them a new heaven and a new earth."[68] Mary began each session with the question, "What is God?" Students who had thought of God as wrathful or a gentle spirit in the sky were pulled away from their perceptions to see God as the "Principle of Being," "the Soul of the Universe."

The basis of her teachings was laid out in the very beginning of *The Science of Man.* She wrote:

> **Question:** What is God?
> **Answer:** *Principle, wisdom, love, and truth.*
>
> **Question:** What is this principle?
> **Answer:** *Life and intelligence.*
>
> **Question:** What is life and intelligence?
> **Answer:** *Soul.*
>
> **Question:** Then, what is God?
> **Answer:** *The Soul of man and the universe.*
>
> **Question:** Is God man?
> **Answer:** *No, they are perfectly distinct and yet united. Soul or God is not man, nor is that which we call Soul in man; while they are ever united as substance and its shadow; Soul the substance, man its shadow.*[69]

In November, Mary held another session. This time, she raised the fee to $300—one-third of the average shoe worker's annual salary. Students thought her classes were worth the price. Mary was devoted to her pupils, and she gave them private instruction in addition to the nightly lessons. When necessary, she met with students who needed extra help and encouragement. One student later recalled, "Every meeting with her was a lesson;

every letter received from her [a lesson as well]. . . . I have never
known of any of her loyal students to complain of not receiving
full value for money paid."[70] Another student declared, "I will
say, and always have said, that her teachings in spiritual science
were beyond any money consideration."[71] At the same time,
Mary was known to reduce the tuition fee or even waive it
altogether for ardent students who could not afford her classes.

Like many new sciences of the time, Mary's teachings met with
considerable criticism. On one occasion, a dissatisfied student
published an article in the *Lynn Transcript* entitled "Moral
Science, alias Mesmerism." Mary wrote a rebuttal to the article
that was published in the same newspaper. The two eventually
faced off in a heated public debate. Mary declared that "Moral
Science belongs to God, and . . . is to put down sin and suffering
through the understanding that God created them not, nor
made he man to be the servant to his body." She concluded by
declaring that she knew nothing more of mesmerism "than does
a kitten."[72]

For almost a year, Mary's practice thrived. But circumstances
struck a sour note in May 1869. Kennedy and Mary had a dis-
agreement about how he was delivering healing to his patients.
Like many healers, Kennedy insisted on rubbing the head of
the afflicted during treatment. Mary believed this practice
contradicted her teachings. When Kennedy refused to change
his methods, the two dissolved their partnership, and Mary left
Massachusetts to visit family and friends in New Hampshire.

Mary returned to her life of shifting from house to house,
spending most of her time revising her book. Finally, on
September 5, 1874, two of Mary's students agreed to pay a
Boston printer to publish her book. In March 1875, she managed
to buy a house at 8 Broad Street in Lynn. To cover expenses, she
rented out most of the lower level. Mary spent the majority of
the day alone in her skylighted third-floor bedroom. There, she
proofread and revised the printer's copy of her manuscript. In
the evenings, Mary taught another class in a small parlor she
reserved for herself on the first floor.

While she put the finishing touches on her book, Mary struggled to come up with a title that pleased her. One night, as Mary lay gazing up at the stars through the skylight, the name came to her. She rose from her bed and walked over to her desk. She wrote the words *Science and Health*. Ever since her childhood days, Mary had dreamed of writing a book. Little did she know that day on the schoolhouse playground that her book would become the foundation of a new religion.

6

Holding the Cross

Every trial of our faith in God makes us stronger.

—Mary Baker Eddy,
Science and Health with Key to the Scriptures

On October 30, 1875, the printer finished a thousand copies of *Science and Health.* In her book, Mary referred to her religion as "Christian Science." She explained that she named it Christian "because it is compassionate, helpful, and spiritual."[73] Her writings referred to God as the "immortal Mind." Conversely, the "mortal mind" is that which sins, suffers, and dies. The physical senses were denoted as "error." To the soul, Mary gave the term "substance"—"Because Soul alone is truly substantial," she explained.[74] Spirit she named "reality," and matter, "unreality." In *Science and Health,* she wrote: "Christian Science is the law of Truth, which heals the sick on the basis of the one Mind or God. It can heal in no other way, since the human, mortal mind so-called is not a healer, but causes the belief in disease."[75]

Through her teachings, Mary conceived of God as wholly good and almighty, the principal source of all that is real. She also referred to God as both father and mother, love, truth, and life. She professed that God is only good, and thus, all that is evil—sin, death, and disease—is a denial of God, and therefore, unreal. In Mary's vision, matter itself was a misconception of reality. Healing constituted the deep spiritual reality of life and of God. Instead of asking God for miracles or simply confessing sins, according to Mary, prayer was a means to revelation. Through prayer, one gains a fuller understanding of love and life.

Mary referenced the New Testament accounts of Jesus's healing as examples of Christian practice. She believed that Christian Science could be proven through demonstration— just as Christ had done. "He proved what he taught," Mary wrote. "This is the Science of Christianity. Jesus *proved* the Principle, which heals the sick and casts out error, to be divine. Few, however, except his students understood in the least his teachings and their glorious proofs."[76]

Some reviews of the book appeared in papers, and many were harsh. One critic advised Mary to "devote her remaining years to healing the sick, and leave the writing of books upon philosophy and religion to others."[77] Other critics enjoyed the book, but doubted its success. As one reviewer wrote: "This book is indeed wholly original, but it will never be read."[78] Bronson Alcott, father of writer Louisa May Alcott, was reasonably impressed with the book and paid a visit to one of Mary's classes.

Mary did not let cruel commentary discourage her. She continued with her healing work and classes at 8 Broad Street. One day, a Mrs. Godfrey and her young daughter came to stay at the house. Her son was a tenant of Mary's. He had sent Mrs. Godfrey a telegram explaining that his wife was ill and needed her help. At the time, Mrs. Godfrey was suffering a serious infection on her finger. Doctors had told her she would risk losing her entire arm if she did not have the finger amputated. But she was a stubborn woman and wanted to give it a chance to heal.

When she arrived, Mrs. Godfrey immediately began making supper. That night, Mary joined them at the dining table. At one point, she reached over and touched Mrs. Godfrey's hand, asking her what was wrong with her finger. The conversation then turned to lighter subjects. The next morning, when Mrs. Godfrey awoke, she noticed that her finger was practically healed. She quickly ran into her son's room and cried, "William, look at my hand!" William took one look at the finger and calmly replied, "Guess Mrs. Glover [Mary] has been trying her works on it."[79] He then went on to tell her about Mary's new method of healing.

At the breakfast table that morning, Mrs. Godfrey asked Mary if she would complete the cure on her hand. Mary agreed, but emphasized that the process would require full reliance on God. Within a week, Mrs. Godfrey's finger looked as though it had never been affected.

Upon returning home to Chelsea, Massachusetts, Mrs. Godfrey openly praised Mary's healing techniques. But her healing was not the last time she would witness them. One night, her daughter, seven-year-old Mary Godfrey, had an attack of croup. Little Mary had suffered these attacks most of her life. Mrs. Godfrey decided to take her daughter to Mary for healing. Wrapping the sick child in a warm blanket, Mrs. Godfrey set out in a snowstorm. When the Godfreys arrived at 8 Broad Street, Mary met them at the door. She cheerfully told the little girl to run upstairs and play. By the time the child had reached the second floor, she was completely healed of her sickness. Mary then turned to the Godfreys and said, "What really needs healing in order to prevent a recurrence of the disease was the parents' fear." [80] Mary encountered many other instances of healing while living at 8 Broad Street, each occurrence demanding the awe of all who witnessed the cure.

MARRIAGE AGAIN

In July 1876, Mary formed the Christian Scientist Association. The goal of the organization was to bring students together for continued education and Christian fellowship. Among Mary's students was newcomer Asa Gilbert Eddy. A true believer in Mary's teachings, Eddy was the first practitioner to declare himself a Christian Scientist on his office sign. Mary and Eddy quickly grew quite close. Six months later, on January 1, 1877, they were married. At age fifty-five, Mary Baker Eddy had become a wife for the third time. Because she was the leader of a growing religion, some people felt her husband might not want to take the passenger seat in their relationship. As it turned out, Eddy was perfectly content to live as his wife's helper. "Mrs. Eddy is the rightful head [of the Christian Science movement]," he said, "and we have never yet succeeded unless she filled that place." [81]

Mary was pleased with her decision to marry and felt it was the best thing for her. But not all of her students approved of the union. In earlier years, Mary had received several marriage proposals and had turned them down for the sake of her work. Some students worried that Eddy might warp his wife's ways of teaching and thinking to reflect his own views and, in so doing, divert her from her mission. Despite the criticisms, Mary stood behind her decision. "I have done what I deem the best thing that could be done under the circumstances," she wrote in a letter two days after her marriage, "and feel sure I can teach my husband up to a higher level of usefulness, to purity, and the higher development of all his *latent noble* qualities of head and heart."[82] Eventually, the controversy subsided. A month after the ceremony, Mary's friends threw a party for her—complete with gifts, wedding cake, and lemonade.

CRITICISM FROM WITHIN

Two former students who strongly objected to Mary's marriage were Daniel Spofford and George Barry. Spofford had unsuccessfully pursued Mary, even filing for divorce from his wife in November 1876 (although the divorce was not granted). At one point, he asked her to marry him. When she refused, he pulled out his pistol and pointed it at her head. Mary calmly asked him to put the gun away, and he obeyed. Spofford's views of Mary's marriage to Eddy probably stemmed from a personal flame. Barry, on the other hand, showed his disapproval by suing Mary three months after her marriage. He claimed that she owed him $2,700 for assigned duties he had performed at 8 Broad Street. Barry's bitterness troubled Mary, especially because, during his years of service, he had called Mary "mother," seeming eager to fill the space of her long lost son. The lawsuit wasn't finally settled until 1879.

Spofford then made a more poignant attack on Mary. Recently appointed her publisher, he was in charge of work surrounding the second edition of *Science and Health*, on which Mary was busy working. Still burning with jealousy and perhaps seeing himself as the rightful cofounder of Christian Science, Spofford looked for a place to vent his rage. He became annoyed by Mary's sluggish progress on her revisions. On May 30, he sent her a heated letter. In it, he wrote: "Nineteen months since the book was first issued and not corrected yet . . . and the 'writing on the wall' is . . . you have proven yourself unworthy to be the standard bearer of Christian Science, and God will remove you from the means for carrying on this work. . . . I propose to carry it alone expecting no one but God to stand by me."[83]

No one followed Spofford, except for a few of his patients. Five days before Christmas, 1877, he was expelled from the Christian Scientist Association. Mary believed Spofford had been led astray by the hypnotic influence of hatred. These events led Mary to ponder the negative effects of mesmerism. She wrote: "Truly the 'Devil and his angels' which are Mesmerism and the messages it sends forth from mortal mind are fighting 'to devour the child as soon as it is born.'"[84]

Mary's troubles continued to gain intensity throughout the following year. The bank in which Gilbert Eddy had invested his savings failed, and with Barry's lawsuit still looming, the Eddys worried that they would be in over their heads. Edward Arens, another of Mary's students, was eager to help his teacher. He suggested that Mary sue past students who had taken advantage of her instruction. Arens helped file suit against Richard Kennedy for unpaid tuition and followed with similar suits against other students. Initially, Kennedy lost the suit, but he appealed the verdict, requesting a trial by jury.

Arens's advice fell far short of his intentions, and the cases ended up doing more harm than good. Stories about the suits hit the newsstands and threatened to discredit Mary's work. However, the Salem witchcraft trial of 1878 stole the thunder from all her other courtroom drama. Miss Lucretia Brown, a Christian Science student and former patient of Spofford's, accused him of using his mesmeric powers to harm her health. The case made front-page news and brought with it extremely bad publicity for the Christian Science movement. Mary tried to remain calm about the situation, and this decision proved wise. The case was dismissed before it could be tried in court on the grounds that it was not in the court's power to restrain Spofford's mind.

Problems continued to pop up in every facet of Mary's life. In late October 1878, the revised edition of *Science and Health* came out, but the printer had been incompetent and the book was practically ruined. This greatly distressed Mary, for she had spent years of work completing the revisions. A few days later, an even greater atrocity came to call at 8 Broad Street. Eddy and Arens were arrested for conspiring to murder Daniel Spofford, who had disappeared on October 15. At the time of the arrest, however, Spofford apparently turned up healthy. Nevertheless, the *Boston Globe* reported: "Finding that they could not dispose of their rival by any process of law, the Eddy combination next resorted to stronger measures . . . visited Boston and bargained with a Portland street 'bummer' to put Dr. Spofford out of the way, in other words, to MURDER HIM IN COLD BLOOD." [85]

Even though Spofford was found unharmed, the conspiracy charges remained in place. Arens and Eddy remained in jail until they were released on $3,000 bail. Reporters took the opportunity to paint the accused as ruthless criminals. Their religion, their home, almost every aspect of their life differed drastically from the norm, which left them prey to gossip and suspicion. During the sensation, Kennedy's appeal came to trial. With newspapers hailing the Eddys as conspirators, no jury would find for the plaintiff, and the early ruling was overturned.

The charges against Eddy were eventually dropped. Apparently, the scheme had been designed to discredit Mary's work. Much of the testimony against Eddy turned out to be perjury. No doubt, through all the slanderous newspaper articles, Christian Science took a damaging blow. Mary must have seen much work ahead in rebuilding the reputation of her religion. She later wrote: "Every trial of our faith in God makes us stronger."[86] By this measure, 1878 was quite a strengthening year for Mary.

7

Strengthening the Christian Science Movement

> *Moral courage is requisite to meet*
> *the wrong and to proclaim the right.*
>
> —Mary Baker Eddy,
> *Science and Health with Key to the Scriptures*

M ary's strength in support of Christian Science never faltered. Even while her husband was under threat of conviction, she gave weekly lectures at the Baptist Tabernacle in Boston. One critic wrote of her: "Though she walked over thorns, her tread was as light as air." [87] Mary never let her personal trials show on her face, even though her heart was heavy with troubles. On the afternoons of her lectures, she dressed smartly in a fur-trimmed velvet coat, a plumed black velvet hat, and gray kid gloves. At age fifty-seven, Mary still possessed exquisite beauty and the glow of youth. One onlooker described her as resembling a queen. Despite the harsh words that had been directed against her, Mary's fiery speeches did not lose their intensity. Her lectures met with loud cheers and applause.

With all the controversy surrounding Christian Science, Mary felt more compelled than ever to establish credibility in the movement. On April 12, 1879, the Christian Scientist Association voted to establish a church, consisting of twenty-six members and led by Mary as pastor and president. Christian Scientists held services in Boston and in members' homes. Their services included a time for silent prayer (which Mary regarded as the only form of sincere prayer), the Lord's Prayer, and a sermon by Mary based on a Bible passage. The sermon was followed by questions and answers. On August 23, the Christian Science movement finally received the recognition it had fought so long and hard to achieve when the state of Massachusetts granted a charter to the Church of Christ, Scientist.

During the winter of 1879–1880, the Eddys lived in Boston, where Mary attended to her growing church. Much to her delight, Mary received a visit from her son, George, who had settled down in Deadwood in the Colorado Territory with his wife and child. This visit was the first time Mary had seen her son in twenty-three years. Their reunion was certainly filled with tears and joy. George stayed a few months with his mother but showed no interest in joining her church.

The Eddys spent the following summer in Concord, New Hampshire, where Mary began work on a third edition of

Science and Health. During their stay, Mary thought hard about ways to strengthen the Christian Science movement. As the church grew in numbers, she felt it necessary to form a solid foundation. An up-to-date version of *Science and Health* was essential, since every member studied the text along with the Bible. But new considerations by lawmakers on regulating medical practice concerned Mary in regard to the future of Christian healing. She wanted to ensure that her method of healing would be recognized as a legitimate form of treatment. After long thought, she determined that the only way to rescue her cause was to establish an accredited institution to teach Christian Science healing methods.

While in Concord, Mary spoke with several medical doctors who thought favorably of Christian Science. When she returned to Massachusetts in the fall, she continued the work of founding a college. According to Massachusetts law, seven or more persons could form a corporation for a charitable, religious, educational, or scientific purpose. Under this broad law, Mary hoped to form her institution. After several entanglements, on January 31, 1881, the Massachusetts Metaphysical College was chartered.

PLAGIARISM

Massachusetts Metaphysical College did not begin operations until the summer of 1881. Until then, Mary was occupied with publishing the third edition of *Science and Health.* This time, she went in search of a trustworthy publisher, and in January 1881, she spoke with John Wilson of the University Press in Cambridge, Massachusetts. Wilson was considered one of the top book manufacturers in the United States. Mary explained that she was unable to supply him with the initial payment required by the University Press, but she was certain that publication of *Science and Health* would prove profitable. Without a moment's hesitation, Wilson agreed to take on the project. He recalled, "I *knew* that the bill would be paid, and I found myself actually eager to undertake the manufacture."[88]

Wilson then asked Mary when she could deliver the manuscript to him. Mary responded by pulling it out of her handbag. Surprised, Wilson asked, "You brought this on the chance of my accepting it?"

"No, not on a chance," Mary replied. "I never doubted." [89]

About this time, some troubles came up concerning Edward Arens—the pupil who had led the Eddys through court cases in 1878. Since his incarceration with Gilbert Eddy, Arens had drifted away from the group. He set up his own healing practice in Boston and began to develop his own ideas and methods. Late in 1880, a pamphlet called *The Science of the Relation Between God and Man and the Distinction Between Spirit and Matter* was published. The work strongly resembled Mary's writings, and upon further examination, it was revealed to be an almost word-for-word rewrite of *The Science of Man* and *Science and Health*.

Mary began questioning people to find out where the work originated. The trail led to Arens and resulted in his expulsion from the Christian Scientist Association. Apparently, Arens had been making copies of Mary's writings, slapping his name on them, and distributing them to his students. When a few of these pupils quit Arens's classes, they ended up as students of Mary's. They explained to her what was happening. After their instruction, Mary had them sign a statement, claiming, "We studied Mrs. Eddy's system of metaphysical healing of Edward J. Arens but he did not understand it as we have since learned. And we did not learn of him how to heal the sick according to metaphysics." [90]

In June 1881, a revised edition of Arens's work was published, this time with a new title: *The Understanding of Christianity, or God*. In this pamphlet, he included an introductory paragraph stating he had "made use of some thoughts contained in a work by Eddy." [91] He went on to say that his changes to the manuscript rendered it wholly original.

On this account, Gilbert Eddy rose to his wife's defense. Eddy was the one who had taught Arens in early 1878, who had trusted him enough to follow him into legal battles, and who had sat in a jail cell with him. All of this disrespect for Mary's work was too much for Eddy to ignore. Eddy made a statement in which he accused Arens of being a plagiarist, and what's more, one who could not keep his story straight. He noted that in one instance, Arens claimed to have learned metaphysics in Germany. The next moment, he said he was one of Mary's students, and in still another case, he asserted that Mary was *his* student. Eddy concluded by stating, "It would require ages and God's mercy to make the ignorant hypocrite who published that pamphlet originate its contents."[92] Mary, too, was greatly distressed by Arens's activities, so much so that she later devoted a section of her autobiography to the subject of plagiarism. In it, she wrote: "A student can write voluminous works on Science without trespassing, if he writes honestly."[93]

For a time, the Eddys wrestled with the decision of whether to take legal action against Arens. Their previous experience in the courtroom left them hesitant to do so. Friends advised Mary not to even bother filing a suit "with such a fool or crazy head." Mary ultimately agreed with their advice and did not take Arens to court. "Keep quiet, don't give things to the Public," she wrote, "work *silently* and . . . vanquish him that way."[94]

On August 17, 1881, the third version of *Science and Health* was published. In this printing, Mary gave a more reasoned and scientific explanation to her teachings. The volume included for the first time her famous "scientific statement of being."[95] Mary's satisfaction in seeing the book in print was short-lived, however. Two months later, she received a shock she would not forget.

LEAVING LYNN

On the evening of October 26, 1881, members of the Christian Scientist Association gathered at 8 Broad Street for a special business meeting. Functions started as usual, but the meeting suddenly took an incredible turn. A letter composed by eight church members, issuing a shocking statement, was read aloud. It stated, in part, ". . . while we acknowledge and appreciate the understanding of Truth imparted to us by our Teacher . . . [due to her] frequent ebullitions of temper, love of money, and the appearance of hypocrisy, *cannot* longer submit to such Leadership."[96] The eight signers—two of whom were Mary's close friends—were not present at the meeting and, up until this time, they had shown no signs of disaffection toward her.

At first, Mary was completely stunned and much too hurt to reply. The twenty members present at the meeting were outraged and drew up the following resolution, which was sent to each of the eight defectors:

> That your unchristian communication of Oct. 21st 81 renders you liable to Church discipline as you have broken our covenant in that you went not to the individual whom you abused. To tell her that you had aught against her. That you had assumed the appearance of full fellowship with her. . . . You are liable to expulsion. You are hereby notified to appear before the Church of Christ (Scientist) . . . on Monday Oct. 31 at 5 P.M. to answer for your unjust proceedings.[97]

After passing the resolution, Mary withdrew from the meeting and the other members quietly exited. She sat alone with her husband and two new students, Abbie Whiting and Calvin Frye. Throughout the night, these four discussed the situation. Mary strongly believed that one member had influenced the others. As the morning began to dawn, Mary, deep in thought, suddenly stood up and began to speak. Her words spilled out of her mouth in fragments, as though they broke from some unconscious stream of thought, and everyone in the room gazed at her in awe. "Is this humiliation, the humility the oppressor would heap upon me!" she exclaimed. "One woe is passed, and behold, another cometh quickly. . . . And the false prophet that is among you shall deceive if possible the very elect, and he shall lead them into forbidden paths. And their feet shall bleed on the jagged rocks." Mary's voice continued to build emotion, and she continued, "I will lift thee up Oh daughter of Zion. And I will make of thee a new nation for thy praise."[98] At the end of her speech, she took a step forward, her eyes staring off into the room. She then seemed to snap back into consciousness, looked around the room, and sat down.

For the next three days, Mary spent hours in prayer and solitude. During this time, she had many visions. She shared these revelations with her closest students. Her pupils were amazed by the words Mary spoke to them. One woman recalled, "We felt that we must take the shoes from off our feet, that we were standing on holy ground."[99]

Mary seemed to rise triumphantly above the crisis, but the immediate rumble was followed by a larger quake. On October 31, the Christian Scientist Association expelled four of its members. In response to this action, several more resigned. Over the next few weeks, more members chose to leave the group. Finally, on November 9, Mary and her loyal students left Lynn in hopes of establishing new roots in Boston—then the nation's cultural and intellectual center. Even after ten years of toil at 8 Broad Street, Mary only looked ahead with hope.

FOUNDATION IN BOSTON

In May 1882, the Eddys rented a four-story gray stone house in Boston. There, they set up the Massachusetts Metaphysical College. The college was the only school of metaphysics ever granted a charter to offer degrees. Mary was the entire faculty. She led classes in obstetrics, metaphysics, and Christian Science. Gilbert Eddy planned to teach alongside her, but he became ill. Normally, Mary helped her husband when he was sick, but Eddy knew the number of tasks she would be neglecting if she took time to care for him. He assured Mary that he could take care of himself.

On June 2, Eddy took an afternoon ride on the horsecars. When he returned, he told Mary that the fresh air and sunshine had done him good. That night, however, he passed away while he was sleeping. Mary was overcome with grief at the death of her husband. At first, she seemed unable to get past losing a devoted coworker and friend. She and two companions went to Vermont, where they stayed for a month in a secluded country home. During her reclusion, she wrote: "I am situated as pleasantly as I can be in the absence of the *one true heart* that has been so much to me. . . . I never shall master this point of missing him all the time . . . [I] am trying as I must—to sever all the chords that bind me to person or things material."[100] For a while, Mary insisted that Eddy was murdered by Arens's mesmeric powers, but an autopsy showed that Eddy's heart had deteriorated from disease.

When Mary returned to Boston, she went back to work with renewed strength. A tragedy that would have slowed many people down instead thrust Mary forward. She immediately began teaching again, and as the numbers of students climbed, so did Mary's enthusiasm. Near the end of October, she wrote: "The ship of science is again walking the wave, rising above the billows, bidding defiance to the flood-gates of error, for God is at the helm."[101]

By the end of 1883, she had taught more than one hundred students. With so many new pupils, Mary kept her eyes open for those with exceptional gifts, who might be suited for additional responsibilities. She encouraged select individuals to hold meetings in their own communities. From time to time, Mary would make surprise visits to these gatherings. She took a seat in the back of the parlor and observed how the student performed. Some Christian Scientist Association members felt that Mary hardened after her husband's death, becoming more demanding and less tolerant. Not all of Mary's followers held this opinion, however. One woman defended Mary, saying, "Did she change? I think not. Some have stated that she became harsh and arbitrary. . . . Mrs. Eddy showed to her early pupils the loving-kindness of a mother . . . and many of her later students have given testimony to the same effect."[102]

Before long, Mary's many responsibilities caught up with her. She wrote that her duties "make me too perplexed too mind-worn often to think—so I would give up writing and at a late hour would crawl into bed to toss all night and half asleep give directions on business *cares* that concern the good cause."[103] Mary called Calvin Frye, a dedicated former student and Christian Science practitioner to help her with her encumbering workload. Frye served the movement as a spokesman, a secretary, and Mary's confidant. He stood by Mary's side for the next twenty-eight years.

Mary soon added the *Journal of Christian Science* to her list of tasks, which she founded in 1883. She served as the editor and principal contributor of this bimonthly publication. The *Journal* had a wide variety of features, including an "Answers and Questions" column, poems, and stories. The back pages held numerous announcements, meetings, services, Christian Science lectures, and a list of Christian Science practitioners. The newspaper circulated west and abroad, bringing fresh students from faraway states and countries. Mary later renamed the publication *The Christian Science Journal*, and over one hundred years later, it is still in circulation.

At age sixty-four, Mary decided to stop treating individual cases and focus instead on teaching and guiding her growing group of followers. The guidance was necessary, as many students had trouble practicing the exact methods Mary taught. This was the case with some Christian Science practitioners in Chicago. Concerned about the welfare of the movement, Mary made a call in the *Journal* for all Christian Scientists to attend the June 1888 meeting in Chicago.

Chicago newspapers announced the coming of the "Boston prophetess," a title that Mary would not have approved of. On her arrival, she received a warm welcome from the citizens but did not plan to make a public speech. On the second day of the convention, four thousand people crowded into the Central Music Hall, where the delegates were meeting. As the Chicago pastor escorted Mary onstage, he whispered to her that she was the advertised speaker of the day. At first, Mary shook her head and told him that she did not wish to speak. But the reverend insisted. Mary at last stepped forward and lifted her eyes up, as if asking for inspiration.

When she concluded her speech, the crowd rose to its feet and rushed the platform, hoping to touch Mary's hand or dress. One reporter noted that listeners "vaulted to the rostrum like acrobats."[104] Mary was escorted through the masses. Along the way, she acknowledged members of the audience. Back at the hotel, Mary withdrew to a private room, where she pondered the events of the afternoon. Although Mary wanted recognition for her religious movement, pandemonium could easily be turned into hostility. Mary knew something had to be done to turn the tides of Christian Science.

8

Starting Again

*Let neither fear nor doubt overshadow
your clear sense and calm trust, that the
recognition of life harmonious . . . can destroy
any painful sense of . . . that which Life is not.*

—Mary Baker Eddy,
Science and Health with Key to the Scriptures

O n February 15, 1889, Mary gave a lecture at Steinway Hall in New York City. The address brought out the same degree of enthusiasm as her speech in Chicago nine months earlier. Newspapers great and small filled their pages with grand descriptions of this lovely, well-dressed sixty-eight-year-old woman and her incredible effect on the crowd. When she returned to Boston, Mary resumed teaching at the Massachusetts Metaphysical College with a class of almost seventy—the largest number of students she ever had in her classroom. The Christian Science movement seemed to be at the height of its success.

By May, a stack of applications towered on Mary's desk, more than she could possibly accept. If her dream had been to see Christian healing grow and prosper, it had become a reality. Yet the September edition of the *Journal* ran an announcement that shocked Christian Scientists everywhere. Mary wrote: "Deeply regretting the disappointment this must occasion, and with grateful acknowledgments to the public, I now close my college." [105]

Her students were stunned by the decision, to say the least. "I supposed the College like the gate to Heaven would always be ajar," one student commented. [106] Their reaction was so emotional that Mary made an effort to keep the school open by appointing a professor to take her place. Her successor was quite capable, and the first class he taught brought tremendous results. Before he could begin, however, Mary wrote him a letter stating that she could not deny God's command, and on October 29, 1889, the school formally closed.

Even after the doors had been shut, Mary's students rallied to convince her to change her mind. A small group of students, including a businessman, decided that they had to speak to Mary in person. They could not understand why she would dissolve the institution when it was just reaching the pinnacle of success. When Mary walked into the room where they were waiting, she began to tell them about the miraculous vision that had led her to close the college. As the students listened in awe, they felt ashamed for wanting to promote their own selfish desires. After Mary finished talking, she asked them why they had come to visit her. They stuttered that it was for no reason in particular.

At the same time, Mary dissolved the Christian Scientist Association. This break was much more difficult for her. The association was made up of intimate friends; through it she nurtured her students, listened to their troubles, and tried to meet their needs. A year later, she resigned as pastor of the Church of Christ, Scientist, in Boston. One month later, she gave control of *The Christian Science Journal* to the national association, created several years earlier. Many of her followers were confused about the sudden change of events. Mary tried to give a somewhat lighthearted explanation in the July 1890 *Journal*. She wrote: "For what purpose has Mrs. Eddy relinquished certain lines of labor in the field of Christian Science? . . . Is she writing her history? or completing her works on the Scriptures? She is doing neither, but is taking a vacation, her first in twenty-five years." [107]

FINDING PLEASANT VIEW

Reasons for her withdrawal had been building over the recent years. Mary's need for a family continued to swell inside of her. But the constant demands of her work left little time to build one. In November 1887, her son, George Glover, his wife, Nellie, and their four children arrived in Boston for a six-month visit. Overly busy at the time, Mary tried to dissuade them from coming, but when they did, she was happy to see her son's family. The Glovers were unsophisticated compared to Mary's circle of friends. In fact, most of the family was illiterate. Accustomed to rural life, they felt out of place in Boston and, after a while, moved back west.

About the time of George's visit, a homeopathic doctor named Ebenezer J. Foster joined one of Mary's classes. Mary developed an affection for the young man, and likewise, he grew devoted to her. Although he was about the same age as George, his personality was quite different. Mary felt a connection with Foster. In November 1888, she legally adopted him as her son, and he changed his name to Foster Eddy.

More than anything, Mary had a desire to get away from society and break free from the pressures and daily demands she had been battling while she contemplated the next steps for her movement. When she dismantled her organization, "there were 250 trained practitioners, 20 churches, 90 societies, and 33 academies of Christian Science."[108] The rapid growth had not only left Mary tired, but also made the organization nearly impossible to regulate. The movement had suffered pressures from society, experienced power struggles from within, and battled attacks from those who falsely claimed to be Christian Scientists. Mary felt that the only way to develop a new direction for her religion was to break it down and build it up again, making it strong enough to endure any challenges that might lie ahead.

Mary moved to Concord and began her fiftieth revision of *Science and Health.* Over the past five years, she had written and published *Historical Sketch of Metaphysical Healing* (1885), *Christian Science: No and Yes* (1887), *Rudiments and Rules of Divine Science* (1887), and *Unity of Good and Unreality of Evil* (1888). In addition to these works, Mary wrote letters, composed articles for the *Journal*, and revised edition after edition of *Science and Health.* Her astounding output of writing was accompanied by a full schedule of teaching and lecturing. All of these activities devoured her time. The only way to give her full attention to the new direction her cause would take was to sever her attachment to this life.

Each revision of *Science and Health* came with tremendous labor pains, and the 1891 edition also posed its challenges. Because Mary no longer taught college classes, she realized that the book would have to be the sole instructor of Christian Science. She spent long hours reworking the text to make it more applicable and easier to understand. Her single-minded dedication to this end sometimes tried the patience of those around her.

By the end of the summer, Mary was ready to begin work on her new church. She focused on leading her organization away from the material. Throughout the past several years, she had discovered the problems associated with building a church on personal popularity. In a letter to a student, she wrote: "Our basis in Science is IMPERSONALITY. . . . You cannot build on *personality* or you build on sand."[109]

Mary needed a peaceful house in the country where she could do her thinking, praying, and writing. A home to her meant more than just four walls. In *Science and Health,* she wrote, "Home is the dearest spot on earth, and it should be the centre, though not the boundary, of the affections."[110] On one occasion, she told her friends, "Home is not a place but a power. We find home when we arrive at the full understanding of God. Home! Think of it! Where sense has no claims and Soul satisfies."[111] For this reason, Mary's standards in finding a house were unmatched by any other.

Mary often went on carriage rides through Concord. On her drives, Mary's attention was frequently drawn to a group of unsightly buildings in need of repair. One day when she was passing the place, the clouds broke and the sunlight showered down on one of the houses. Mary felt that it was a vision from heaven, and she immediately arranged to buy the house. It was a farmhouse just outside of the city.

Before moving in, however, Mary made some renovations. She instructed workers to build a tower where she would have her study and a scenic view in several directions. She also added a three-tiered veranda that ran the entire length of the house. There, she later enjoyed afternoon respite on a swing chair. She also directed landscaping around the house. She told a friend, "There should be about it [the house] noble trees, beautiful shrubbery, flowers, vines clambering over the house, and a rose garden."[112] Mary inspected all the work she requested, which, at times, frustrated the workers. She set unusually high standards— but was rarely wrong in her observations.

On June 20, 1892, Mary moved into her new home. She stood on the veranda and looked off into the distance. From her porch, she could see the distant Bow Hills, where seventy years ago her life had begun in a respected Puritan home. Mary named her new home Pleasant View, because to her everything about the place appeared to be just that—pleasant.

BUILDING THE MOTHER CHURCH

Before moving into Pleasant View, Mary was engaged in discussions with members of the Boston congregation of Christian Scientists regarding some legal business surrounding a deed. The deed was for a three-sided plot of land in the high-society Back Bay area of Boston. On this plot, Mary had a vision of building a Christian Science church. She decided against organizing the church under a state charter, and her plans caused some legal entanglements.

Mary's lawyers failed to find a law that would allow her to erect a church without a charter. Exasperated, she went to a judge who also said he knew of no law that would accommodate her. She asked him "upon what was human law based?"

He thought for a moment about her question and replied, "Upon the divine law. But," he continued, "if the Massachusetts abstracter of law can find no such statute, how can I?"

"God has somewhere provided such a law," Mary told him, "and I know you can find it." [113]

Sure enough, three days later, the judge reported to Mary that he had discovered what she was looking for in an obscure Massachusetts law. She quickly purchased the land, and for one dollar, she transferred the title to a new Christian Science board of directors. According to the deed of trust, if for any reason the board failed to follow all of Mary's detailed stipulations, the property would revert back to her or her heirs. A few weeks later, the Mother Church, the First Church of Christ, Scientist, was established. At first, thirty-two members joined the congregation, but that number quickly grew. The members of any branch church could also hold membership in the Mother Church. Mary's new organization was finally taking shape.

The physical state of the Mother Church was moving slowly, though. Mary kept a careful watch over the construction and interjected her thoughts freely. In the beginning, the board delayed construction as the first frost of winter was near. Annoyed by the hesitancy to what she deemed divine instruction, Mary chided, "Why in the name of *common sense* do you not lay the foundation of our church as GOD BIDS YOU, AT ONCE?"[114] Twelve days later, when no progress had been made, she urged them again, instructing them to "thrust in the spade Oct. 1st, 1893."[115]

Still concerned about the coming frost, the board refused to obey Mary's orders. After a month passed, still with no work done, Mary wrote another letter. "I protest against this delay to have the *foundation built*," she said. "Also I warn you against the mental argument for this to be done when the *frost comes!*"[116] Two days later, work began for setting the foundation—before the freeze.

At the end of October 1894, the board projected six more months of work before the church building would be completed. When Mary heard this news, she insisted that the church be finished by the end of the year. In order to meet this deadline, she suggested that the board give up some of its "gods," meaning the mosaic flooring, the marble and onyx decorations, and the silk walls for the "Mother's Room." "I would rather," she argued, "see 5000 hearers in a plain wooden Tabernacle listening to the Scriptures and Science & Health than pride and contracted walls hemming in 1200 hungry hearers."[117]

All through December, the building rattled with constant activity. On Saturday night, December 29, the building was finished, and workmen laid the sidewalk in front of the church, covering it with a tent to keep the cement from freezing. Inside, a troop of Christian Scientists, armed with pails, mops, and brooms, cleaned the auditorium. At exactly midnight, all work ceased. The church was completed and ready for the Sunday morning service, just as Mary had instructed.

The auditorium held 1,500 people. In order to accommodate all attendees, five dedication services had to be held throughout the day. Remembering what had happened in Chicago and New York, Mary chose not to attend the dedication. Under her new movement, she did not want church members to look at her as the base of Christian Science. Mary finally stepped into the Mother Church on a Monday afternoon in April. She did not let anyone know of her visit. Alone, she stood in the auditorium and gazed with amazement at the beauty of this church. The colored light from the stained glass windows fell softly on the rose plush pews. The neutral walls stood tall with their frescoed borders, dotted with silver lamps.

On a rainy night twenty-seven years ago, Mary had been sent out of a house just forty miles away, without money, without friends, without shelter, with only a vision of something great. Standing beneath the sunburst in the center of the dome, she paused to reflect on her life. She then slowly moved toward the marble steps that led to the readers' platform and knelt down on the lowest step in silent prayer.

9

Life at Pleasant View

*All my work, all my efforts,
all my prayers and tears are for humanity,
and the spread of peace and love among mankind.*

—Mary Baker Eddy,
quoted in the *New York American*

At Pleasant View, Mary ran both the grounds and the household with both economic efficiency and strict organization. For herself, she was no different and kept a rigid schedule that varied only by season. She rose as early as six or seven every morning. Her maid brought a breakfast of cornmeal mush and milk to her room. While Mary enjoyed her meal, the maid set out her clothes and brought in a pitcher of warm water, which Mary used to bathe.

After eating breakfast and getting dressed, Mary met her staff, which eventually numbered in the teens, in the study for a meeting of prayer and discussion. She sat down at her desk and randomly opened her Bible or *Science and Health*. Whatever page the book opened to was the topic of that morning's devotion. She then came downstairs, where she went over household duties for the day in fine detail. At precisely noon, dinner (as Mary called it) was served.

Although Mary enjoyed simple foods, she was very particular about the quality of the meal. The cook always kept an extra dinner on hand, in case the lady of the house found the soup too salty, the baked potatoes too hard, or the sponge cake too heavy. Mary's favorite foods were cream of tomato soup, salt pork, and, above all, ice cream. One of the noises tolerated at Pleasant View was the sound of the ice-cream churn turning.

Every day after lunch, Mary took a ride in one of her carriages. Her daily ride was one of her greatest pleasures. As she passed through the streets of Concord, she relaxed in her seat, greeting the townspeople and children as they came out of their houses to watch her ride past. For her rides, Mary always dressed in her finest silk gloves, fur-lined coats, and fancy bonnets. Most days, she went out on the ride alone, but on occasion Calvin Frye accompanied her—smartly dressed in his uniform and top hat.

On her return from her drive, she spent the afternoon with her secretary, tending to correspondence, discussing organizational issues, and receiving visitors. At six in the evening, she sat down to supper. Following the meal, she often enjoyed fellowship with her associates, simply chatting or perhaps gathering around the piano for a sing-along. Other nights, Mary enjoyed the peaceful solitude out on the veranda, gently pushing herself in her swing.

Her first two years at Pleasant View were spent overseeing construction of the Mother Church. After the building was completed, however, the workload continued to be "severe and unrelenting."[118] Every room in the house was equipped with a bell that connected to Mary's room. She expected each staff member to respond promptly to his or her sequence of rings. Domestic helpers worked from dawn until dusk, seven days a week, and rarely did they sleep through the night undisturbed. The secretaries and watchers had less physical strains, but they still carried a heavy burden of stress, and were more likely to fail under the scrutinizing eye of their leader. Watchers had the important duty of aiding Mary in the middle of the night if she was unable to sleep, had a nightmare, or was ill. On these occasions, watchers were called to ease her pain or help her regain a right mind. If within fifteen minutes Mary did not feel any relief, she dismissed the watcher with a stern reprimand. Much to the amazement of her staff, on many of these sleepless nights, Mary emerged in the morning bright, cheerful, and full of energy.

Mary accepted few excuses for being absent when she rang the bell, and on one particular occasion, even death was not a sufficient excuse. One night, Mary rang repeatedly for Frye. When he did not respond, staff members rushed to his room and found him slumped over, stiff, cold, and lifeless in his chair. Mary got out of bed and made her way to Frye's room in her nightdress. She immediately bent over him and began shouting statements of truth in his ear: "Wake up and be the man God made!" For over an hour, she continued to call to him. At last, Frye stirred and began to mumble broken phrases, "Don't call me back. . . . Let me go. . . . I am so tired." To these words, Mary replied that she would indeed continue to call him out of the dream-state in which he was caught—that he loved life and its activities too much to fall asleep.[119]

Through her extreme organization and rigid schedule, Mary built the foundation for the future of Christian Science. She wanted to be certain that her exact teachings would be followed by all her church members. Although she sometimes seemed harsh in her words, her actions were driven by love for her students, church, and mission.

THE LAST CLASS

In spring 1897, Mary published *Miscellaneous Writings*, an edited compilation of addresses, sermons, essays, and articles she had previously written. She considered the publication of such monumental importance that she banned all other forms of Christian Science teaching for an entire year. Over the past decade, there had been an increased outpouring of false material under the name of Christian Science. In order to do away with the inadequate literature, Mary wanted to use an entirely fresh composition as the basis of instruction. As another way of renewing momentum in the church, she decided in November 1898 that she would teach one more class. Almost ten years had passed since the doors of Massachusetts Metaphysical College closed. Knowing that the announcement of another class would bring hundreds of applications, Mary chose to keep the decision to herself and to handpick her students. The class she chose was uniquely balanced in age and gender.

On Tuesday, November 15, Mary wrote out seventy brief telegrams and letters, inviting the individuals to meet her at 4:00 P.M. the following Sunday at the Christian Science Hall in Concord. There, she informed them, they would receive a great blessing. Mary marked the envelopes confidential and sent them out to be delivered. No one else was informed of the event.

On the day of the meeting, Mary's swift step and ease of movement did not seem to be that of a seventy-seven-year-old woman. This appearance was the first time in years that many of the class members had been in her presence, and some had actually never seen her before. The students marveled at her graceful gestures, clear voice, and delicate figure. As always, Mary was dressed in fashionable attire—down to her fur cape and white kid gloves.

Mary chose to run the two sessions of classes in a question-and-answer format. She had a clear and important message to teach her students, and she openly corrected them when necessary. Yet her goal was to inspire the class, not to rebuke and condemn, and she succeeded. In her new class, she presented Christian Science in positive terms. She made no mention of her long-detested crusade against Malicious Animal Magnetism. Illuminating enemies, real or suspected, was a thing of the past. Many students found this change the most impressive of her new teaching methods. Another point Mary stressed was that members should be careful not to make her into some kind of god. She instructed them to detach Christian Science from her person and to restrain from making an idol out of her. After explaining the dangers of "material personality," Mary solemnly added, "I trust that no personal sense of me will ever stand between you and Christian Science." [120] As the years went on, many critics accused Christian Scientists of deifying their leader. Mary continually felt compelled to deny and discourage this belief. In a private statement to Foster Eddy, she said, "I am a human being and should be treated as such, and spoken of as such, until I find my place outside of this state of being. . . . In the flesh I am not what I desire to be. . . . I am not a heathen concept or idol." [121]

THE WOODBURY CASE

Josephine Curtis Woodbury has come to be known as one of the most bizarre and famous characters in Christian Science history. Woodbury not only made Mary miserable but also had an impact on her religious thinking. The events that Woodbury played out led Mary to place an increasing emphasis on purity of thought in healing, and ultimately explained why she believed that the future of Christian Science belonged in the hands of men.

Throughout the 1880s, Woodbury was a successful healer who openly praised Mary as her leader. Her work brought with it a number of devoted followers. In 1886, she established her own Christian Science academy in Boston. She had little success as a healer in Boston, and healing is what earned money in Christian Science. Without a steady income, Woodbury journeyed out of town, first to Maine and later to Denver, Colorado. Woodbury's followers were an interesting group. They differed drastically from Mary's rule-abiding students. According to one account, they were visited by inspirations, revelations, and premonitions, "and spoke of God as coming and going, agreeing and disagreeing. . . . Some of them affected cell-like sleeping-chambers with white walls, bare except for a picture of Christ. They longed for martyrdom, and made adventures out of the most commonplace occurrences." [122]

Although Woodbury preached sexual abstinence, she was married and openly engaged in numerous extramarital affairs. On one occasion, Mary confronted Woodbury and her lover. When the two claimed that they were acting out roles from the Book of Revelation, Mary rebuked them and told them to separate from each other forever. Despite her apparent guilt, Woodbury continued to profess abstinence, and when she gave birth to an illegitimate child in 1888, she hailed it as an immaculate conception. She even went so far as to baptize her son "The Prince of Peace," present him as an object of worship to her students, and attribute the event to Mary—who Woodbury claimed possessed knowledge of a secret doctrine that repeats the virgin birth with Christian Science women of exceptional purity. She later recanted her claim and wrote a letter of apology to Mary.

For a while, Mary hoped Woodbury would be able to rehabilitate herself, and she extended all the love of a mother to a sick child. But Woodbury continued in her loose behavior, often talking about sexual acts to her followers. When Mary heard about this, she was outraged, especially since Christian Science preaches absolute purity of thought. "How dare you," Mary wrote. "How dare you in the sight of God and with your character behind the curtain, and your own students ready to lift it on you, pursue a path perilous?" [123] Shortly after this letter in 1897, Woodbury was expelled from the Christian Scientist Association and excommunicated from the Mother Church.

Humiliated by this treatment, Woodbury vowed revenge. She set to slandering Mary at every corner she turned. She joined a former student of Quimby's named Julius Dress in reviving the claim that Mary had plagiarized Quimby's writings and ideas. Woodbury even went so far as to plant an article in the Chicago *Inter Ocean*, in which she stated that Chicago Christian Scientists doubted whether Mary were even alive. In response, the *Boston Journal* printed an interview with Mary Baker Eddy. The article began, "Am I alive? Why, I haven't felt more sound for forty years." [124]

Six weeks later, Woodbury brought a suit for libel against Mary and other related suits against the Mother Church, the board of directors, the board of trustees, and other church officials. [125] The suits were based on Mary's 1899 Communion message to the church, several weeks after Woodbury's husband died. In her speech, Mary quoted parts of Revelation, but her use of the text seemed to be pointed directly at Woodbury. "This woman," she said, "drunk with the wine of her fornication, would enter even the church—the body of Christ, Truth; and, retaining the heart of the harlot and the purpose of the destroying angel. . . . The Babylonish woman is fallen, and who should mourn over the widowhood of lust, of her that 'is become the habitation of devils, and the hold of every foul spirit . . . ?'" [126]

Woodbury's attorney was Fredrick W. Peabody, a shrewd Boston lawyer, who would have a tremendous influence on Mary's life and reputation over the next twenty-five years. In this case, the plaintiff requested damages of $150,000. Peabody's swift legal actions, his decision to file six separate suits in both New Hampshire and Massachusetts, and his ingenious tactic of naming not only Mary, but also the board of directors and other church officers made many at the Mother Church and at Pleasant View tremble in uncertainty. Peabody, who, like his client, was also suffering financial strain, hoped the suits would win him both money and public success. He was confident that he would win in court, but his case was not as solid as he thought.

For his argument, Peabody attacked the core of the Christian Science religion, asserting that the defendant claims to be the "equal of Jesus Christ." He went on to point out that Christian

Scientists believe that "sickness, suffering, and death of another human being [may be caused by] mental effort."[127] Therefore, Mary had caused anguish and suffering to his client when she gave her Communion speech.

The judge in the case did not look favorably on Peabody's tactics. Citizens of the United States had the right to think and believe as they wished, as long as they behaved within the confines of the law. To attack a religious group for its doctrines or a religious leader for his or her teachings was incredibly unpopular in American society, and freedom of religion was well protected by the judicial system.[128] By attempting to discredit Christian Science as his foundation, Peabody fatally weakened his case.

By this point in Mary's career, she could afford to appoint good counsel. The defense lawyers gathered statements from Woodbury's followers to counter her testimony that she was "a person of chaste life and conversation."[129] They also set to work on Mary's Communion address, in an effort to prove that she was not referring to Woodbury in her message. In this task, they had two things going for them: One was that Mary never actually mentioned Woodbury's name when she was speaking. Secondly, Revelation is a somewhat mystical book, not simple in its interpretations. In the end, Mary's legal team easily won in court. The judge dismissed the case in the first week without having to call any of Mary's witnesses. On hearing the judge's decision, Peabody swelled with rage and bitterness. Over the next ten years, he became the most violent and most quotable opponent of Christian Science.[130]

After the Woodbury case, Mary began to wonder about the future of the church. Advancing in age, she would need to designate a leader to follow her. Her experiences with Josephine Woodbury greatly tipped her inclination. In an interview with Joseph Clarke of the *New York Herald*, Mary revealed, "No present change is contemplated in the rulership. You would ask, perhaps, whether my successor will be a woman or a man. I can answer that. It will be a man."[131]

10

The Final Years

God is my life.

—Mary Baker Eddy

The amazing success of Christian Science coupled with its in-and-out court dramas made the religion and Mary herself prime material for the sensationalist newspapers of the time. Joseph Pulitzer, owner of the New York *World*, had a nose for a good story like no other. Starting in 1904, word was out that *McClure's Magazine* was preparing a lengthy and critical biography of Mary that would appear in the fall of 1906. Not wanting Sam McClure to get the breaking scoop on Christian Science, Pulitzer dispatched his own team of reporters up to Concord, New Hampshire, to get the story for themselves. Pulitzer was no fan of Christian Science. He put absolutely no stock in mental healing, and the fact that his primary publishing rival, William Randolph Hearst, supported the religion only intensified his desire to expose this "mumbo-jumbo" science.

Experienced *World* reporters Slaght and Lithchild immediately set to work in Concord. They dug through local financial records, scoured the town for gossip, and exchanged information with the *McClure's Magazine* team, which was also active in the area. Their investigation kept them busy for most of the summer of 1906. On a Sunday afternoon in October, Slaght and Lithchild visited Pleasant View and asked to see Calvin Frye. They informed Frye that they had interviewed several people who had once known Mary Baker Eddy, including Richard Kennedy and Daniel Spofford. According to numerous sources, Mrs. Eddy was dead or incapacitated. In order to disprove these rumors, the journalists insisted that they had to see Mrs. Eddy for themselves. They added that they would bring along John Kent, the former Concord High School principal and a vocal opponent of Mary, to identify her.

Confronted with this serious ultimatum, Frye agreed to try to persuade Mrs. Eddy to meet with the two men. The next day, when Mary returned from her drive, Frye told her about the previous day's events. He explained that he felt obligated to accept the interview. Mary agreed and immediately sent for the two reporters and Kent. When the men arrived, Mary held out her hand to Kent and commented that she hoped he would soon regain his position at the school. This statement proved that she knew who he was and remembered his recent professional setbacks. The meeting only lasted a few minutes. As the men left Pleasant View, the *World* reporters even commented to the staff how wonderful Mary looked for her age. In a letter to Frederick Peabody, Kent verified that the woman he met was definitely Mrs. Eddy. For the most part, the interview went well, and Mary felt relieved that the rumors would now be squelched.

The reality turned out to be something quite different, however. Searching for a sensational news item, the reporters prepared a long, fabricated story that appeared on the front page of the Sunday, October 28 edition:

MRS. MARY BAKER G. EDDY DYING
FOOTMAN AND "DUMMY" CONTROL HER
Founder of X Science Suffering from Cancer and Nearing
Her End, Is Immured at Pleasant View. While Another
Woman Impersonates Her in Streets of Concord.[132]

In the article, the reporters claimed Mary was dying of cancer and was receiving secret visits from a physician. "Mrs. Eddy looked more dead than alive," they reported. "She was a skeleton, her hollow cheeks thick with red paint. . . . As the visitors were hurried from the room, Mrs. Eddy, surrounded by attendants, was sinking helpless into a pillowed chair."[133]

Mary's withdrawal from public circles and her increased emphasis on downplaying her personal importance in the church lent credibility to the article. Other than her staff, few people had seen her recently, and her absence at the dedication of the Mother Church was duly noted. All this aside, the newspaper account was hard for some to swallow. Mary was a well-respected citizen in Concord, and she was New Hampshire's most famous resident.

Mary was no stranger to unfavorable press, but the bold and widespread article distressed her somewhat. She decided to subject herself to yet another interview, this time with the intentions of negating the *World* report. The meeting took place on Tuesday, October 30. Representatives from more than eight leading newspapers attended. On her way out to her carriage, the reporters asked her three presubmitted questions.

The first reporter asked, "Are you in perfect bodily health?"

"Indeed I am," Mary replied.

"Have you any other physician than God?"

Mary took a step forward and responded, "No physician but God. His everlasting arms are around me, and that is enough."

"Do you take a daily drive?"

"Yes," she quickly said, and walked down the front walk.[134]

After the brief interview, the group watched Mary get into her carriage and ride away.

Any hopes to defend herself were quickly dashed. The interview was a disaster, much too short to prove or disprove anything. The reporters were left to fill in the details with their own journalistic embellishments. When the articles came out, reports varied. One writer claimed that, as Mary walked out of the house, she was "shaking and trembling, she tottered forward, clutching the curtains with palsied hands and paused swaying in the door."[135] If anything, the second interview supported the *World* article and placed Mary in an even more feeble light. Pulitzer was pleased with the outcome of this critical interview, and more importantly, he was encouraged to continue his crusade against Christian Science.

NEXT FRIENDS SUIT

Pulitzer saw Mary as a poor, pathetic, old woman, with too much money for her own good. He was convinced that she was mentally unable to handle the affairs of her estate and was being taken advantage of by her personal aide—namely, Calvin Frye. In order to drum up publicity and support his newspaper's claims, he decided to take legal action. Pulitzer did not have the legal standing to bring his own suit, but he knew of one man who certainly did—George Glover. If he could hunt down

Mary's son and perhaps some other relatives, he might be able to convince them to investigate the state of her affairs.

In order to carry out this grand scheme, Pulitzer needed the right lawyer. While Slaght and Lithchild were in Concord digging up gossip on Mary, they met a former U.S. senator from New Hampshire, William Eaton Chandler, a fierce opponent of the Christian Science movement. In addition to being a brilliant lawyer, Chandler had a reputation for picking quarrels and enjoying a fight. One of the people against whom he had publicly taken a stand was Mary Baker Eddy. By November 1906, Chandler had agreed to Pulitzer's offer and began working full-time on what would later be called the Next Friends suit.

Over the years, the relationship between Mary and her son had become strained. In 1889, George's daughter, Evelyn, became deathly ill. George wrote to his mother in despair, begging her to treat Evelyn personally. By this time, Mary had given up performing healings and felt strongly enough about sticking to her decision that she refused to make an exception. In 1893, George brought his sick wife unannounced to Concord, again pleading with his mother to cure her. Not only did Mary refuse to treat Nellie's illness, but she would not even see her son for six weeks. When she finally did take the time to see him, it was for a brief twenty-five-minute visit. Although Nellie soon recovered, that was not the case for Evelyn. She continued to suffer from various ailments until she died in 1904 at the age of twenty-three. These events no doubt soured George's feelings toward his mother.

In addition to personal matters, George was constantly facing financial problems. Although Mary repeatedly came to his aid and tried her best to help him become self-sufficient, George had poor management skills and an attraction to gold prospecting, which always seemed to lead him back into debt. By 1906, the Glover family was again in dire straits. When Chandler wrote in a letter to George that Mary "MAY BE detained in the custody of strangers against her will" [136] and her staff might be taking advantage of her financially, George jumped at the opportunity to come to his mother's rescue, especially if it might prove lucrative for him. However, George also expressed a concern that if his mother *were* mentally competent, his actions might lead her to disinherit him.

To assess the situation himself, George and his family visited Mary at Pleasant View. When they entered Mary's room, she was busy with work and did not acknowledge them for several minutes. As soon as she finished what she was doing, she rose to her feet and affectionately embraced them. Mary asked George what brought him to Concord. He replied business. Accepting his vague response, Mary told him about all the recent events in the press. The family then talked about his finances. He told her that he owned several mining properties out west and only needed the capital to develop them. As she had done many times before, Mary said he would never make any money in mining and should just give it up. As a rebuttal, George shared with her his very different vision.

After their visit, the Glovers reported back to Chandler. Several remarks from Mary convinced George that she was, in fact, losing her mind. When he commented on the earthquake and fire in San Francisco and events surrounding President Theodore Roosevelt, Mary acted as though she knew nothing about them. She said she no longer had time to read the papers. During their talk, Mary claimed that two men from Lead had stolen her will, forcing her to make another. She also said that a Southern man who had given her a pair of horses wanted to kill her.

As strange as these comments seemed, they were not merely the ramblings of a senile woman. Mary's busy schedule left her with little time. Keeping up with current events probably seemed frivolous compared with her much larger mission. But Chandler investigated her other statements. He found that in 1901, her will was really lost and a new one replaced it in 1903. However, he failed to find any validity to the claim that two men had stolen it. As for the horses, an admirer of Mary's had given her a gift of two expensive horses. Unfortunately, the horses were not well broken, and on one occasion, they gave Mary quite a scare during a carriage ride. Mary may have thought the horses were an attempt on her life, but Chandler thought the accusation was a stretch. After reviewing Glover's report, he decided it was time to take action.

VICTORY IN COURT

At 5:30 P.M. on March 1, 1907, Chandler's associate in Concord personally informed Mary's lawyer, Frank S. Streeter, that he had filed a bill in equity petitioning that "a receiver or receivers be appointed to take possession of all the property" of Mrs. Eddy.[137] Streeter was extremely annoyed by the news. He explained that the timing of the suit was unfortunate for all parties involved, as just half an hour earlier he had sent a messenger to Washington to inform George that Mrs. Eddy had set up a $125,000 trust fund for the benefit of his family. Streeter asked if it might be possible to contact Chandler by phone and sort the whole matter out without taking it to court. Before he could even finish speaking, the press arrived and made the call impossible. Apparently, Chandler's associate had alerted them to the matter.

Streeter called back his messenger, and George would not find out about the trust until June. The trust Mary had established would have paid the Glovers $1,500 a year for the rest of their lives, and would also have taken care of their taxes, insurance, and repair bills on their house in Lead. The children also would have received $500 a year for the term of the trust. This money would have more than ensured the Glovers' comfort for years to come. But with the suit filed and the trust offer retracted, it was too late.

Chandler diligently researched the history of Mary's estate in an effort to find some instance where her trustees had mishandled her funds. Much to his dismay, he was unable to find any such evidence. He turned then to the question of her sanity. Chandler was thoroughly convinced that the eighty-five-year-old woman had long been clinically insane, a condition that may have resulted from her fall in 1866. With this direction, he hoped to prove that she had been unable to make any sound legal decisions for the previous forty or more years. These decisions would have included the greatest one of all—her transfer of the Mother Church property. According to Chandler, the title of this property should rightfully have been transferred to Mary's son, her next friends (those who should be looking after her best interests), upon her death.

In court, Chandler reasoned that Mary was legally incompetent because she believed herself to be a messenger of God. In other words, she was insane because she had founded Christian Science. Chandler wrote: "Christ supposedly healed the sick. . . . Then the art died away and remained dead till 1866 when Mary Baker Glover Patterson discovered it. God, Christ, Mrs. Eddy! It is all a delusion as the facts show." [138] Apparently, Chandler did not make the connection that it was only through founding Christian Science that she had acquired the property he hoped to gain for his client.

On the side of the defense, Streeter invited a reputable firm of accountants to audit Mary's books for the fourteen years prior to March 6, 1907. They testified first that Mary was not worth millions as had been reported in the *World*, but rather owned around $900,000. Second, her bookkeeper—Calvin Frye—had made "all kinds and classes of clerical errors," but all of them amounted to $677.41 against himself.[139] As Mary had often remarked, she could easily have found a more competent bookkeeper, but not one nearly as honest.

Mary helped her own defense by writing a letter to the judge on May 16. Instead of dictating the letter, which she had often done, she wrote it in her own hand. This point discredited reports of "palsied" hands. In the letter, she defended her decision to appoint a board of trustees to handle her estate. She explained that her reason for doing so was because of the "increasing demands upon my time labors and thought and yearning for more peace" and not because her friends were trying to steal her money. In reference to the character of her trustees, she stated, "I selected said trustees because I had implicit confidence in each one of them as to honesty and business capacity."[140]

The judge ruled that he would interview Mary himself and decide whether or not she was mentally competent. He visited her at Pleasant View to make his assessment. During his examination, the judge found nothing faulty about Mary's sanity. On his way out the door, he commented that Mary had a mind like a steel trap. Within a week, the Next Friends suit was over. Mary had emerged the victor. For the plaintiffs, the verdict was a shocking defeat. George Glover gained nothing from the case except more debt and a marred relationship with his mother. Even the public had been drawn to Mary's side through the whole ordeal, for what Mary thought seemed like the very first time. Newspapers across the country declared the result a "victory of justice." [141]

CHESTNUT HILL

During and after the Next Friends suit, Mary continued her projects with the Christian Science movement. She wrote letters to colleagues about a proposed edition of *Science and Health* in German, among other works. Although the court had finally come down on Mary's side, all the drama surrounding the incident did take a heavy toll on her. As much as she loved Pleasant View, she wanted to find more peaceful surroundings. She asked her staff to find a new country home for her in Boston. In early October, they purchased a twenty-five-room house in Chestnut Hill and immediately set to getting it ready for Mary's arrival.

On January 26, 1908, Mary left Pleasant View at the same time she would have normally taken her daily drive. The carriage took her to the railway station, where she secretly boarded a special train bound for Boston. Despite her precautions, a worker from the Concord railway station alerted the Boston press that Mrs. Eddy was on her way. When the driver pulled up in front of Mary's new home, she was met by a mob of reporters. She turned to her escort and said, "John, can you get me into the house?" [142] In reply, he picked her up in his arms and carried her laughing through the front door. Her amusement quickly turned to sadness, however, when she began to look around. Pleasant View had been modest in size and accommodations compared with this elaborate mansion. Mary had been very specific about what the new home should be like and how the rooms should be arranged, especially her bedroom. She wanted her old room to be reproduced exactly. She even went so far as to say, "I want a window in my room like the one here. It relieves my *lonely hours*."[143] When her staff asked her if it could be larger, she agreed without enthusiasm. Her new room was double the size of her old one. When she sat down in her chair, the window she had requested was positioned too high for her to look out. She sank into tears and mumbled, "Oh splendid misery, splendid misery."[144]

Immediately, Mary made plans to redecorate this new "big barn of a place,"[145] as she called it. She moved her room to the third floor, where the rooms were cozy and had a nice view. Three weeks later, the house had been remodeled to Mary's approval. The second-floor rooms were converted to Pleasant View dimensions, and the windows were lowered. The slope of the driveway was changed to give the house more privacy, and a large tree was cut down so Mary could look out at nearby homes.

At age eighty-seven, Mary was not yet ready to retire from her work completely. On July 28, 1908, she took what she later recorded as "the greatest step forward since I gave *Science and Health* to the world."[146] She wrote a letter to the board of directors, asking them to begin work on a daily newspaper called *The Christian Science Monitor*. "This must be *done* without fail," she concluded.[147]

The immediate reaction of the board was one of shock. They had just finished making arrangements for a new publishing house to be built. They tried to put a temporary stall on the project. In August, the publishing society moved into its new facilities. As soon as Mary got word of the move, she again wrote to the board: "It is my request that you start a daily newspaper at once. . . . Let there be no delay."[148]

Mary planned the newspaper to be competition for the low-quality sensationalist newspapers of the time. The *Monitor* would not carry Christian Science articles exclusively, but rather would

The front page of the first issue of *The Christian Science Monitor*, which was published on November 25, 1908, gives an idea of the broad sampling of topics that the newspaper intended to cover.

present news on current events. In order to get the project moving, the publishing house needed new machinery and more room. Mary searched the ranks of Christian Scientists for experienced journalists and editors to staff the paper. Only three and a half months later, on November 25, the first twelve-page issue of *The Christian Science Monitor* appeared on newsstands.

Increasingly, Mary declined to answer the board of directors'

MARY BAKER EDDY

Mary Baker Eddy was the youngest child of Abigail Ambrose Baker and Mark Baker (seen here). Mark Baker was a hardworking and respected member of the community of Bow, New Hampshire, where the family originally lived. He served as a clerk for the local Congregational church and worked for the town council. Mary inherited much of her religious zeal from her father.

This photograph of Mary Baker was taken around the time of her marriage to George Washington Glover, in 1843. Although her father was at first opposed to the courtship, he eventually relented and allowed the young couple to be married in the family parlor.

Dr. Phineas P. Quimby was famous for his ability to heal illness through what he referred to as a "mind cure." An early devotee of Quimby's method, Mary Baker Eddy used Quimby's teachings as a foundation for her later development of the faith-based healings of Christian Science.

Seen here dressed in a military uniform in a photograph taken around 1863, George Glover was Mary Baker Eddy's only child. Although she was devoted to her son, financial circumstances prevented her from raising him herself for large portions of his childhood. He spent most of his youth living with the Cheneys, trusted friends of Mary's.

Because her many years of constant hard work were
wearing on her health and emotional state, Mary Baker
Eddy wanted a country home where she could rest and
work in peace. Her hopes were fulfilled when she found
Pleasant View, her home in Concord, New Hampshire
(seen here).

Mary Baker Eddy loved her home at Pleasant View—particularly her cozy study (seen here) with its many windows from which she could see the surrounding landscape that included a distant view of her childhood hometown.

Even as she got older, Mary Baker Eddy refused to slow down when it came to her work with the religion she had founded. In fact, she was eighty-seven when she decided it was time to begin publishing a daily newspaper—*The Christian Science Monitor*. Seen here in a photograph from around 1908 (the year the paper was first issued) are a set of *Monitor* delivery trucks waiting beside the original publishing building at 107 Falmouth Street in Boston.

Although Mary Baker Eddy did not attend the inaugural ceremonies celebrating the completion of the Mother Church building in Boston, she was integral in its design and planning. It remains a symbol of her life and legacy.

Often a controversial figure, Mary Baker Eddy nonetheless had a profound influence on religious thinking both in her own time and in the many years since her death in 1910. Even today, the Church of Christ, Scientist, that Eddy founded remains a popular faith, both in the United States and even abroad.

questions concerning church business. Instead, she encouraged them to go to God for guidance. In November 1909, she printed a statement in the *Journal* that, even given her advanced age, stunned many of her followers. She wrote: "I hereby publicly declare I am not personally involved in the affairs of the church in any other way than through my written and published rules."[149]

Over the past months, Mary had suffered occasional attacks of illness. She wanted to spend her last days relaxed and in peace. She wrote less and spent more time on her afternoon drives. In the evenings, Mary enjoyed sitting on her porch swing gazing up at the stars. Near the end of November, she came down with a severe cold. On Thursday, December 1, 1910, she went out for her carriage ride as usual. When she returned, one of her staff members carried her up to her room. After he set her down in a chair, she asked for a piece of paper. On it, she wrote her last words: "God is my life."[150] The next day, Mary was too weak to get out of bed, although she continued to have rational conversations with her watchers. During the night of December 2, Mary Baker Eddy slipped quietly away in her sleep. She was eighty-nine years old.

Even in death, Mary continued to amaze people with her beauty and countenance. The medical examiner stated, "What struck me most as I looked into the dead face was its extraordinary beauty. . . . I do not recall ever seeing in death before a face which bore such a beautifully tranquil expression."[151] Likewise, the undertaker was surprised at the youthful condition of her body. "The tissues were remarkably normal," he reported. "The skin was well preserved, soft, pliable, smooth and healthy. I do not remember having found the body of a person of such advanced age in so good a physical condition."[152]

On Sunday, December 4, many sad faces lined the birch pews of the Mother Church. Tears dripped down the cheeks of the people as they mourned the death of their beloved leader. As they exited the church, many wondered what would come next.

They need not have worried. Today, almost a century after Mary Baker Eddy's death, the church she founded still maintains a following all over the world.

APPENDIX

PREFACE TO *SCIENCE AND HEALTH*

To those leaning on the sustaining infinite, today is big with blessings. The wakeful shepherd beholds the first faint morning beams, ere cometh the full radiance of a risen day. So shone the pale star to the prophet-shepherds; yet it traversed the night, and came where, in cradled obscurity, lay the Bethlehem babe, the human herald of Christ, Truth, who would make plain to benighted understanding the way of salvation through Christ Jesus, till across a night of error should dawn the morning beams and shine the guiding star of being.

The Wisemen were led to behold and to follow this daystar of divine Science, lighting the way to eternal harmony. The time for thinkers has come. Truth, independent of doctrines and time-honored systems, knocks at the portal of humanity. Contentment with the past and the cold conventionality of materialism are crumbling away. Ignorance of God is no longer the stepping-stone to faith. The only guarantee of obedience is a right apprehension of Him whom to know aright is Life eternal. Though empires fall, "the Lord shall reign forever."

A book introduces new thoughts, but it cannot make them speedily understood. It is the task of the sturdy pioneer to hew the tall oak and to cut the rough granite. Future ages must declare what the pioneer has accomplished. Since the author's discovery of the might of Truth in the treatment of disease as well as of sin, her system has been fully tested and has not been found wanting; but to reach the heights of Christian Science, man must live in obedience to its divine Principle. To develop the full might of this Science, the discords of corporeal sense must yield to the harmony of spiritual sense, even as the science of music corrects false tones and gives sweet concord to sound.

Theology and physics teach that both Spirit and matter are real and good, whereas the fact is that Spirit is good and real, and matter is Spirit's opposite. The question, What is Truth, is answered by demonstration, by healing both disease and sin; and this demonstration shows that Christian healing confers the most health and makes the best men. On this basis Christian Science will have a fair fight. Sickness has been combated for centuries by doctors using material remedies; but the question arises, Is there less sickness because of these practitioners? A vigorous "No" is the response deducible from two connate facts, the reputed longevity of the Antediluvians, and the rapid multiplication and increased violence of diseases since the flood.

In the author's work, RETROSPECTION AND INTROSPECTION, may be found a biographical sketch, narrating experiences which led her, in the year 1866, to the discovery of the system that she denominated Christian Science. As early as 1862 she began to write down and give to friends the results of her Scriptural study, for the Bible was her sole teacher; but these compositions were crude, the first steps of a child in the newly discovered world of Spirit.

She also began to jot down her thoughts on the main subject, but these jottings were only infantile lispings of Truth. A child drinks in the outward world through the eyes and rejoices in the draught. He is as sure of the world's existence as he is of his own; yet he cannot describe the world. He finds a few words, and with these he stammeringly attempts to convey his feeling.

Later, the tongue voices the more definite thought, though still imperfectly. So was it with the author. As a certain poet says of himself, she "lisped in numbers, for the numbers came." Certain essays written at that early date are still in circulation among her first pupils; but they are feeble attempts to state the Principle and practice of Christian healing, and are not complete nor satisfactory expositions of Truth.

Today, though rejoicing in some progress, she still finds herself a willing disciple at the heavenly gate, waiting for the Mind of Christ. Her first pamphlet on Christian Science was copyrighted in 1870; but it did not appear in print until 1876, as she had learned that this Science must be 1876, as she had learned that this Science must be demonstrated by healing, before a work on the subject could be profitably studied. From 1867 until 1875, copies were, however, in friendly circulation.

Before writing this work, SCIENCE AND HEALTH, she made copious notes of Scriptural exposition, which have never been published. This was during the years 1867 and 1868. These efforts show her comparative 1867 and 1868. These efforts show her comparative ignorance of the stupendous Life-problem up to that time, and the degrees by which she came at length to its solution; but she values them as a parent may treasure the memorials of a child's growth, and she would not have them changed. The first edition of SCIENCE AND HEALTH was published in 1875. Various books on mental healing have since been issued, most of them incorrect in theory and filled with plagiarisms from SCIENCE AND HEALTH. They regard the human mind as a healing agent, whereas this mind is not a factor in the Principle of Christian Science. A few books, however, which are based on this book, are useful.

The author has not compromised conscience to suit the general drift of thought, but has bluntly and honestly given the text of Truth. She has made no effort to embellish, elaborate, or treat in full detail so infinite a theme. By thousands of well-authenticated cases of healing, she and her students have proved the worth of her teachings. These cases for the most part have been abandoned as hopeless by regular medical attendants. Few invalids will turn to God till all physical supports have failed, because there is so little faith in His disposition and power to heal disease.

The divine Principle of healing is proved in the personal experience of any sincere seeker of Truth. Its purpose is good, and its practice is safer and more potent than that of any other sanitary method. The unbiased Christian thought is soonest touched by Truth, and convinced of it. Only those quarrel with her method who do not understand her meaning, or discerning the truth, come not to the light lest their works be reproved. No intellectual proficiency is requisite in the learner, but sound morals are most desirable. Many imagine that the phenomena of physical healing in Christian Science present only a phase of the action of the human mind, which action in some unexplained way results in the cure of disease. On the contrary, Christian Science rationally explains that all other pathological methods are the fruits of human faith in matter, faith in the workings, not of Spirit, but of the fleshly mind which must yield to Science.

The physical healing of Christian Science results now, as in Jesus' time, from the operation of divine Principle, before which sin and disease lose their reality in human consciousness and disappear as naturally and as necessarily as darkness gives place to light and sin to reformation. Now, as then, these mighty works are not supernatural, but supremely natural. They are the sign of Immanuel, or "God with us," a divine influence ever present in human consciousness and repeating itself, coming now as was promised aforetime, to preach deliverance to the captives [of sense], and recovering of sight to the blind, to set at liberty them that are bruised. When God called the author to proclaim His Gospel to this age, there came also the charge to plant and water His vineyard.

The first school of Christian Science Mind-healing was started by the author with only one student in Lynn, Massachusetts, about the year 1867. In 1881, she opened the Massachusetts Metaphysical College in Boston, under the seal of the Commonwealth, a law relative to colleges having been passed, which enabled her to get this institution chartered for medical purposes. No charters were granted to Christian Scientists for such institutions after 1883, and up to that date, hers was the only College of this character which had been established in the United States, where Christian Science was first introduced.

During seven years over four thousand students were taught by the author in this College. Meanwhile she was pastor of the first established Church of Christ, Scientist; President of the first Christian Scientist Association, convening monthly; publisher of her own works; and (for a portion of this time) sole editor and publisher of the Christian Science Journal, the first periodical issued by Christian Scientists. She closed her College, October 29, 1889, in the height of its prosperity with a deep lying conviction that the next two years of her life should be given to the preparation of the revision of SCIENCE AND HEALTH, which was published in 1891. She retained her charter, and as its President, reopened the College in 1899 as auxiliary to her church. Until June 10, 1907, she had never read this book throughout consecutively in order to elucidate her idealism.

In the spirit of Christ's charity, as one who "hopeth all things, endureth all things," and is joyful to bear consolation to the sorrowing and healing to the sick, she commits these pages to honest seekers for Truth.

MARY BAKER EDDY

APPENDIX

MESSAGE TO THE MOTHER CHURCH
JUNE 1901

BELOVED brethren, to-day I extend my heart-and-hand-fellowship to the faithful, to those whose hearts have been beating through the mental avenues of mankind for God and humanity; and rest assured you can never lack God's outstretched arm so long as you are in His service. Our first communion in the new century finds Christian Science more extended, more rapidly advancing, better appreciated, than ever before, and nearer the whole world's acceptance.

To-day you meet to commemorate in unity the life of our Lord, and to rise higher and still higher in the individual consciousness most essential to your growth and usefulness; to add to your treasures of thought the great realities of being, which constitute mental and physical perfection. The baptism of the Spirit, and the refreshment and invigoration of the human in communion with the Divine, have brought you hither.

All that is true is a sort of necessity, a portion of the primal reality of things. Truth comes from a deep sincerity that must always characterize heroic hearts; it is the better side of man's nature developing itself.

As Christian Scientists you seek to define God to your own consciousness by feeling and applying the nature and practical possibilities of divine Love: to gain the absolute and supreme certainty that Christianity is now what Christ Jesus taught and demonstrated—health, holiness, immortality. The highest spiritual Christianity in individual lives is indispensable to the acquiring of greater power in the perfected Science of healing all manner of diseases.

We know the healing standard of Christian Science was and is traduced by trying to put into the *old* garment the new-old cloth of Christian healing. To attempt to twist the fatal magnetic element of human will into harmony with divine power, or to substitute good words for good deeds, a fair seeming for right being, may suit the weak or the worldly who find the standard of Christ's healing too high for them. Absolute certainty in the practice of divine metaphysics constitutes its utility, since it has a divine and demonstrable Principle and rule—if some fall short of Truth, others will attain it, and these are they who will adhere to it. The feverish pride of sects and systems is the death's-head at the feast of Love, but Christianity is ever storming sin in its citadels, blessing the poor in spirit and keeping peace with God.

What Jesus' disciples of old experienced, his followers of to-day will prove, namely, that a departure from the direct line in Christ costs a return under difficulties; darkness, doubt, and unrequited toil will beset all their returning footsteps. Only a firm foundation in Truth can give a fearless wing and a sure reward.

The history of Christian Science explains its rapid growth. In my church of over twenty-one thousand six hundred and thirty-one communicants (two thousand four hundred and ninety-six of whom have been added since last November) there spring spontaneously the higher hope, and increasing virtue, fervor, and fidelity. The special benediction of our Father-Mother God rests upon this hour: "Blessed are ye when men shall revile you, and persecute you, and shall say all manner of evil against you falsely, for my sake."

APPENDIX

GOD IS THE INFINITE PERSON

We hear it said the Christian Scientists have no God because their God is not a person. Let us examine this. The loyal Christian Scientists absolutely adopt Webster's definition of God, "A Supreme Being," and the Standard dictionary's definition of God, "The one Supreme Being, self-existent and eternal." Also, we accept God, emphatically, in the higher definition derived from the Bible, and this accords with the literal sense of the lexicons: "God is Spirit," "God is Love." Then, to define Love in divine Science we use this phrase for God—divine Principle. By this we mean Mind, a permanent, fundamental, intelligent, divine Being, called in Scripture, Spirit, Love.

It is sometimes said: "God is Love, but this is no argument that Love is God; for God is light, but light is not God." The first proposition is correct, and is not lost by the conclusion, for Love expresses the nature of God; but the last proposition does not illustrate the first, as light, being matter, loses the nature of God, Spirit, deserts its premise, and expresses God only in metaphor, therefore it is illogical and the conclusion is not properly drawn. It is logical that because God is Love, Love is divine Principle; then Love as either divine Principle or Person stands for God—for both have the nature of God. In logic the major premise must be convertible to the minor.

In mathematics four times three is twelve, and three times four is twelve. To depart from the rule of mathematics destroys the proof of mathematics; just as a departure from the Principle and rule of divine Science destroys the ability to demonstrate Love according to Christ, healing the sick; and you lose its susceptibility of scientific proof.

God is the author of Science—neither man nor matter can be. The Science of God must be, is, *divine*, predicated of Principle and demonstrated as divine Love; and Christianity is divine Science, else there is no Science and no Christianity.

We understand that God is personal in a scientific sense, but is not corporeal nor anthropomorphic. We understand that God is not finite; He is the infinite Person, but not three persons in one person. Christian Scientists are theists and monotheists. Those who misjudge us because we understand that God is the infinite One instead of three, should be able to explain God's personality rationally. Christian Scientists consistently conceive of God as One because He is infinite; and as triune, because He is Life, Truth, Love, and these three are one in essence and in office.

If in calling God "divine Principle," meaning divine Love, more frequently than Person, we merit the epithet "godless," we naturally conclude that he breaks faith with his creed, or has no possible conception of ours, who believes that three persons are defined strictly by the word Person, or as One; for if Person is God, and he believes three persons constitute the Godhead, does not Person here lose the nature of one God, lose monotheism, and become less coherent than the Christian Scientist's sense of Person as one divine infinite triune Principle, named in the Bible Life, Truth, Love?—for each of these possesses the nature of all, and God omnipotent, omnipresent, omniscient.

Man is person; therefore divine metaphysics discriminates between God and man, the creator and the created, by calling one the divine Principle of all. This suggests another query: Do Christian Scientists believe in personality? They do, but their personality is defined spiritually, not materially—by Mind, not by matter. We do not blot out the material race of Adam, but leave all sin to God's fiat—self-extinction, and to the final manifestation of the real spiritual man and universe. We believe, according to the Scriptures, that God is infinite Spirit or Person, and man is His image and likeness: therefore man reflects Spirit, not matter.

We are not transcendentalists to the extent of extinguishing anything that is real, good, or true; for God and man in divine Science, or the logic of Truth, are coexistent and eternal, and the nature of God must be seen in man, who is His eternal image and likeness.

The theological God as a Person necessitates a creed to explain both His person and nature, whereas God explains Himself in Christian Science. Is the human person, as defined by Christian Science, more transcendental than theology's three divine persons, that live in the Father and have no separate identity? Who says the God of theology is a Person, and the God of Christian Science is not a person, hence no God? Here is the departure. Person is defined differently by theology, which reckons three as one and the infinite in a finite form, and Christian Science, which reckons one as one and this one *infinite*.

Can the infinite Mind inhabit a finite form? Is the God
of theology a finite or an infinite Person? Is He one
Person, or three persons? Who can conceive either of
three persons as one person, or of three infinites? We
hear that God is not God except He be a Person, and this
Person contains three persons: yet God must be One
although He is three. Is this pure, specific Christianity?
and is God in Christian Science no God because He is not
after this model of personality?

The logic of divine Science being faultless, its consequent
Christianity is consistent with Christ's hillside sermon,
which is set aside to some degree, regarded as impracticable
for human use, its theory even seldom named.

God is Person in the infinite scientific sense of Him, but
He can neither be one nor infinite in the corporeal or anthropomorphic sense.

Our departure from theological personality is, that God's
personality must be as infinite as Mind is. We believe in
God as the infinite Person; but lose all conceivable idea
of Him as a finite Person with an infinite Mind. That
God is either inconceivable, or is manlike, is not my sense
of Him. In divine Science He is "altogether lovely," and
consistently conceivable as the personality of infinite Love,
infinite Spirit, than whom there is none other.

Scholastic theology makes God manlike; Christian
Science makes man Godlike. The trinity of the Godhead
in Christian Science being Life, Truth, Love, constitutes
the individuality of the infinite Person or divine intelligence
called God.

Again, God being infinite Mind, He is the all-wise, all-knowing, all-loving Father-Mother, for God made man in His own image and likeness, and made them male and female as the Scriptures declare; then does not our heavenly Parent—the divine Mind—include within this Mind the thoughts that express the different mentalities of man and woman, whereby we may consistently say, "Our Father-Mother God"? And does not this heavenly Parent know and supply the differing needs of the individual mind even as the Scriptures declare He will?

Because Christian Scientists call their God "divine Principle," as well as infinite Person, they have not taken away their Lord, and know not where they have laid Him. They do not believe there must be something tangible to the personal material senses in order that belief may attend their petitions to divine Love. The God whom all Christians now claim to believe in and worship cannot be conceived of on that basis; He cannot be apprehended through the material senses, nor can they gain any evidence of His presence thereby. Jesus said, "Thomas, because thou hast seen me, thou hast believed: blessed are they that have not seen, and yet have believed."

CHRIST IS ONE AND DIVINE

Again I reiterate this cardinal point: There is but one Christ, and Christ is divine—the Holy Ghost, or spiritual idea of the divine Principle, Love. Is this scientific statement more transcendental than the belief of our brethren, who regard Jesus as God and the Holy Ghost as the third *person* in the Godhead? When Jesus said, "I and my Father are one," and "my Father is greater than I," this was said in the sense that one ray of light is light, and it is one with light, but it is not the full-orbed sun. Therefore we have the authority of Jesus for saying Christ is not God, but an impartation of Him.

Again: Is man, according to Christian Science, more transcendental than God made him? Can he be too spiritual, since Jesus said, "Be ye therefore perfect, even as your Father which is in heaven is perfect"? Is God Spirit? He is. Then is man His image and likeness, according to Holy Writ? He is. Then can man be material, or less than spiritual? As God made man, is he not wholly spiritual? The reflex image of Spirit is not unlike Spirit. The logic of divine metaphysics makes man none too transcendental, if we follow the teachings of the Bible.

The Christ was Jesus' spiritual selfhood; therefore Christ existed prior to Jesus, who said, "Before Abraham was, I am." Jesus, the only immaculate, was born of a virgin mother, and Christian Science explains that mystic saying of the Master as to his dual personality, or the spiritual and material Christ Jesus, called in Scripture the Son of God and the Son of man—explains it as referring to his eternal spiritual selfhood and his temporal manhood. Christian Science shows clearly that God is the only generating or regenerating power.

The ancient worthies caught glorious glimpses of the Messiah or Christ, and their truer sense of Christ baptized them in Spirit—submerged them in a sense so pure it made seers of men, and Christian healers. This is the "Spirit of life in Christ Jesus," spoken of by St. Paul. It is also the mysticism complained of by the rabbis, who crucified Jesus and called him a "deceiver." Yea, it is the healing power of Truth that is persecuted to-day, the

spirit of divine Love, and Christ Jesus possessed it, prac-
tised it, and taught his followers to do likewise. This
spirit of God is made manifest in the flesh, healing and sav-
ing men,—it is the Christ, Comforter, "which taketh away
the sin of the world;" and yet Christ is rejected of men!

The evil in human nature foams at the touch of good;
it crieth out, "Let us alone; what have we to do with
thee, . . . ? art thou come to destroy us? I know thee who
thou art; the Holy One of God." The Holy Spirit takes
of the things of God and showeth them unto the creature;
and these things being spiritual, they disturb the carnal
and destroy it; they are revolutionary, reformatory, and—
now, as aforetime—they cast out evils and heal the sick.
He of God's household who loveth and liveth most the
things of Spirit, receiveth them most; he speaketh wisely,
for the spirit of his Father speaketh through him; he
worketh well and healeth quickly, for the spirit giveth him
liberty: "Ye shall know the truth, and the truth shall
make you free."

Jesus said, "For all these things they will deliver you
up to the councils" and "If they have called the master
of the house Beelzebub, how much more shall they call
them of his household? Fear them not therefore: for
there is nothing covered, that shall not be revealed."

Christ being the Son of God, a spiritual, divine emana-
tion, Christ must be spiritual, not material. Jesus was
the son of Mary, therefore the son of man only in the
sense that man is the generic term for both male and
female. The Christ was not human. Jesus was human,
but the Christ Jesus represented both the divine and the

human, God and man. The Science of divine metaphysics removes the mysticism that used to enthrall my sense of the Godhead, and of Jesus as the Son of God and the son of man. Christian Science explains the nature of God as both Father and Mother.

Theoretically and practically man's salvation comes through "the riches of His grace" in Christ Jesus. Divine Love spans the dark passage of sin, disease, and death with Christ's righteousness,—the atonement of Christ, whereby good destroys evil,—and the victory over self, sin, disease, and death, is won after the pattern of the mount. This is working out our own salvation, for God worketh with us, until there shall be nothing left to perish or to be punished, and we emerge gently into Life everlasting. This is what the Scriptures demand—faith according to works.

After Jesus had fulfilled his mission in the flesh as the Son of man, he rose to the fulness of his stature in Christ, the eternal Son of God, that never suffered and never died. And because of Jesus' great work on earth, his demonstration over sin, disease, and death, the divine nature of Christ Jesus has risen to human apprehension, and we see the Son of man in divine Science; and he is no longer a material man, and mind is no longer in matter. Through this redemptive Christ, Truth, we are healed and saved, and that not of our selves, it is the gift of God; we are saved from the sins and sufferings of the flesh, and are the redeemed of the Lord.

THE CHRISTIAN SCIENTISTS' PASTOR

True, I have made the Bible, and "Science and Health

with Key to the Scriptures," the pastor for all the churches
of the Christian Science denomination, but that does not
make it impossible for this pastor of ours to preach! To
my sense the Sermon on the Mount, read each Sunday
without comment and obeyed throughout the week, would
be enough for Christian practice. The Word of God is a
powerful preacher, and it is not too spiritual to be prac-
ical, nor too transcendental to be heard and understood.
Whosoever saith there is no sermon without personal
preaching, forgets what Christian Scientists do not, namely,
that God is a Person, and that he should be willing to hear
a sermon from his personal God!

But, my brethren, the Scripture saith, "Answer not a
fool according to his folly, lest thou also be like unto him."
St. Paul complains of him whose god is his belly: to
such a one our mode of worship may be intangible, for it
is not felt with the fingers; but the spiritual sense drinks
it in, and it corrects the material sense and heals the sinning and the sick. If St. John should tell that man that
Jesus came neither eating nor drinking, and that he baptized with the Holy Ghost and with fire, he would naturally reply, "That is too transcendental for me to believe
or for my worship. That is Johnism, and only Johnites
would be seen in such company." But this is human: even
the word Christian was anciently an opprobrium;—
hence the Scripture, "When the Son of man cometh, shall
he find faith on the earth?"

Though a man were begirt with the Urim and Thum-
mim of priestly office, yet should not have charity, or should
deny the validity and permanence of Christ's command to
heal in all ages, he would dishonor that office and misin-

terpret evangelical religion. Divine Science is not an interpolation of the Scriptures, it is redolent with health, holiness, and love. It only needs the prism of divine Science, which scholastic theology has obscured, to divide the rays of Truth, and bring out the entire hues of God. The lens of Science magnifies the divine power to human sight; and we then see the allness of Spirit, therefore the nothingness of matter.

NO REALITY IN EVIL OR SIN

Incorporeal evil embodies itself in the so-called corporeal, and thus is manifest in the flesh. Evil is neither quality nor quantity: it is not intelligence, a person or a principle, a man or a woman, a place or a thing, and God never made it. The outcome of evil, called sin, is another nonentity that belittles itself until it annihilates its own embodiment: this is the only annihilation. The visible sin should be invisible: it ought not to be seen, felt, or acted: and because it ought not, we must know it is not, and that sin is a lie from the beginning,—an illusion, nothing, and only an assumption that nothing is something. It is not well to maintain the position that sin is sin and can take possession of us and destroy us, but well that we take possession of sin with such a sense of its nullity as destroys it. Sin can have neither entity, verity, nor power thus regarded, and we verify Jesus' words, that evil, *alias* devil, sin, is a lie—therefore is nothing and the father of nothingness. Christian Science lays the axe at the root of sin, and destroys it on the very basis of nothingness. When man makes something of sin it is either because he fears it or loves it. Now, destroy the conception of sin as something, a reality, and you destroy the fear and the love of it; and sin disappears. A man's fear, unconquered, conquers him, in whatever direction.

In Christian Science it is plain that God removes the punishment for sin only as the sin is removed—never punishes it only as it is destroyed, and never afterwards; hence the hope of universal salvation. It is a sense of sin, and not a sinful soul, that is lost. Soul is immortal, but sin is mortal. To lose the sense of sin we must first detect the claim of sin; hold it invalid, give it the lie, and then we get the victory, sin disappears, and its unreality is proven. So long as we indulge the presence or believe in the power of sin, it sticks to us and has power over us. Again: To assume there is no reality in sin, and yet commit sin, is sin itself, that clings fast to iniquity. The Publican's wail won his humble desire, while the Pharisee's self-righteousness crucified Jesus.

Do Christian Scientists believe that evil exists? We answer, Yes and No! Yes, inasmuch as we do know that evil, as a false claim, false entity, and utter falsity, does exist in thought; and No, as something that enjoys, suffers, or is *real*. Our only departure from ecclesiasticism on this subject is, that our faith takes hold of the fact that evil cannot be made so real as to frighten us and so master us, or to make us love it and so hinder our way to holiness. We regard evil as a lie, an illusion, therefore as unreal as a mirage that misleads the traveller on his way home.

It is self-evident that error is not Truth; then it follows that it is untrue; and if untrue, unreal; and if unreal, to conceive of error as either right or real is sin in itself. To be delivered from believing in what is unreal, from fearing it, following it, or loving it, one must watch and pray that he enter not into temptation—even as one guards his door against the approach of thieves. Wrong is thought before it is acted; you must control it in the first instance, or it will control you in the second. To overcome all wrong, it must become unreal to us: and it is good to know that wrong has no divine authority; therefore man is its master. I rejoice in the scientific apprehension of this grand verity.

The evil-doer receives no encouragement from my declaration that evil is unreal, when I declare that he must awake from his belief in this awful unreality, repent and forsake it, in order to understand and demonstrate its unreality. Error uncondemned is not nullified. We must condemn the claim of error in every phase in order to prove it false, therefore unreal.

The Christian Scientist has enlisted to lessen sin, disease, and death, and he overcomes them through Christ, Truth, teaching him that they cannot overcome us. The resistance to Christian Science weakens in proportion as one understands it and demonstrates the Science of Christianity.

A sinner ought not to be at ease, or he would never quit sinning. The most deplorable sight is to contemplate the infinite blessings that divine Love bestows on mortals, and their ingratitude and hate, filling up the measure of wickedness against all light. I can conceive of little short of the old orthodox hell to waken such a one from his deluded sense; for all sin is a deluded sense, and dis-ease in sin is better than ease. Some mortals may even need to hear the following thunderbolt of Jonathan Edwards:—

"It is nothing but God's mere pleasure that keeps you from being this moment swallowed up in everlasting destruction. He is of purer eyes than to bear to have you in His sight. There is no other reason to be given why you have not gone to hell since you have sat here in the house of God, provoking His pure eyes by your sinful, wicked manner of attending His solemn worship. Yea, there is nothing else that is to be given as a reason why you do not at this moment drop down into hell, but that God's hand has held you up."

FUTURE PUNISHMENT OF SIN

My views of a future and eternal punishment take in a poignant present sense of sin and its suffering, punishing itself here and hereafter till the sin is destroyed. St. John's types of sin scarcely equal the modern nondescripts, whereby the demon of this world, its lusts, falsities, envy, and hate, supply sacrilegious gossip with the verbiage of hades. But hatred gone mad becomes imbecile—outdoes itself and commits suicide. Then let the dead bury its dead, and surviving defamers share our pity.

In the Greek *devil* is named *serpent—liar—the god of this world*; and St. Paul defines this world's god as dishonesty, craftiness, handling the word of God deceitfully. The original text defines *devil* as *accuser, calumniator*; therefore, according to Holy Writ these qualities are objectionable, and ought not to proceed from the individual, the pulpit, or the press. The Scriptures once refer to an evil spirit as *dumb*, but in its origin evil was loquacious, and was supposed to outtalk Truth and to carry a most vital point. Alas! if now it is permitted license, under sanction of the gown, to handle with garrulity age and Christianity! Shall it be said of this century that its greatest discoverer is a woman to whom men go to mock, and go away to pray? Shall the hope for our race commence with one truth told and one hundred falsehoods told about it?

The present self-inflicted sufferings of mortals from sin, disease, and death should suffice so to awaken the sufferer from the mortal sense of sin and mind in matter as to cause him to return to the Father's house penitent and saved; yea, quickly to return to divine Love, the author and finisher of our faith, who so loves even the repentant prodigal—departed from his better self and struggling to return—as to meet the sad sinner on his way and to welcome him home.

MEDICINE

Had not my first demonstrations of Christian Science or metaphysical healing exceeded that of other methods, they would not have arrested public attention and started the great Cause that to-day commands the respect of our best thinkers. It was that I healed the deaf, the blind, the dumb, the lame, the last stages of consumption, pneumonia, etc., and restored the patients in from one to three interviews, that started the inquiry, What is it? And when the public sentiment would allow it, and I had overcome a difficult stage of the work, I would put patients into the hands of my students and retire from the comparative ease of healing to the next more difficult stage of action for our Cause.

From my medical practice I had learned that the dynamics of medicine is Mind. In the highest attenuations of homoeopathy the drug is utterly expelled, hence it must be mind that controls the effect; and this attenuation in some cases healed where the allopathic doses would not.

When the "mother tincture" of one grain of the drug was attenuated one thousand degrees less than in the beginning, that was my favorite dose.

The weak criticisms and woeful warnings concerning Christian Science healing are less now than were the sneers forty years ago at the medicine of homoeopathy; and the medicine of Mind is more honored and respected to-day than the old-time medicine of matter. Those who laugh at or pray against transcendentalism and the Christian Scientist's religion or his medicine, should know the danger of questioning Christ Jesus' healing, who administered no remedy apart from Mind, and taught his disciples none other. Christian Science seems transcendental because the substance of Truth transcends the evidence of the five personal senses, and is discerned only through divine Science.

If God created drugs for medical use, Jesus and his disciples would have used them and named them for that purpose, for he came to do "the will of the Father. " The doctor who teaches that a human hypothesis is above a demonstration of healing, yea, above the grandeur of our great master Metaphysician's precept and example, and that of his followers in the early centuries, should read this Scripture: "The fool hath said in his heart, There is no God."

The divine Life, Truth, Love—whom men call God—
is the Christian Scientists' healer; and if God destroys the
popular triad—sin, sickness, and death—remember it
is He who does it and so proves their nullity.
Christians and clergymen pray for sinners; they believe
that God answers their prayers, and that prayer is a divinely
appointed means of grace and salvation. They believe
that divine power, besought, is given to them in times of
trouble, and that He worketh with them to save sinners.
I love this doctrine, for I know that prayer brings the
seeker into closer proximity with divine Love, and thus
he finds what he seeks, the power of God to heal and to
save. Jesus said, "Ask, and ye shall receive;" and if not
immediately, continue to ask, and because of your often
coming it shall be given unto you; and he illustrated his
saying by a parable.

The notion that mixing material and spiritual means,
either in medicine or in religion, is wise or efficient, is
proven false. That animal natures give force to character
is egregious nonsense—a flat departure from Jesus'
practice and proof. Let us remember that the great Metaphysician healed the sick, raised the dead, and com-
manded even the winds and waves, which obeyed him
through spiritual ascendency alone.

MENTAL MALPRACTICE

From ordinary mental practice to Christian Science is a
long ascent, but to go from the use of inanimate drugs to
any susceptible misuse of the human mind, such as mesmerism, hypnotism, and the like, is to subject mankind
unwarned and undefended to the unbridled individual
human will. The currents of God flow through no such
channels.

APPENDIX

The whole world needs to know that the milder forms
of animal magnetism and hypnotism are yielding to its
aggressive features. We have no moral right and no
authority in Christian Science for influencing the thoughts
of others, except it be to serve God and benefit mankind.
Man is properly self-governed, and he should be guided
by no other mind than Truth, the divine Mind. Christian
Science gives neither moral right nor might to harm either
man or beast. The Christian Scientist is alone with his
own being and with the reality of things. The mental
malpractitioner is not, cannot be, a Christian Scientist; he
is disloyal to God and man; he has every opportunity to
mislead the human mind, and he uses it. People may
listen complacently to the suggestion of the inaudible
falsehood, not knowing what is hurting them or that they
are hurt. This mental bane could not bewilder, darken, or
misguide consciousness, physically, morally, or spiritually,
if the individual knew what was at work and his power
over it.

This unseen evil is the sin of sins; it is never forgiven.
Even the agony and death that it must sooner or later
cause the perpetrator, cannot blot out its effects on himself till he suffers up to its extinction and stops practising
it. The crimes committed under this new-old *régime* of
necromancy or diabolism are not easily reckoned. At
present its mystery protects it, but its hidden modus and
flagrance will finally be known, and the laws of our land
will handle its thefts, adulteries, and murders, and will
pass sentence on the darkest and deepest of human
crimes.

Christian Scientists are not hypnotists, they are not
mortal mind-curists, nor faith-curists; they have faith,

but they have Science, understanding, and works as well. They are not the *addenda*, the *et ceteras*, or new editions of old errors; but they are what they are, namely, students of a demonstrable Science leading the ages.

QUESTIONABLE METAPHYSICS

In an article published in the *New York Journal*, Rev.— writes: "To the famous Bishop Berkeley of the Church of England may be traced many of the ideas about the spiritual world which are now taught in Christian Science."

This clergyman gives it as his opinion that Christian Science will be improved in its teaching and authorship after Mrs. Eddy has gone. I am sorry for my critic, who reckons hopefully on the death of an individual who loves God and man; such foreseeing is not foreknowing, and exhibits a startling ignorance of Christian Science, and a manifest unfitness to criticise it or to compare its literature. He begins his calculation erroneously; for Life is the Principle of Christian Science and of its results. Death is neither the predicate nor postulate of Truth, and Christ came not to bring death but life into the world. Does this critic know of a better way than Christ's whereby to benefit the race? My faith assures me that God knows more than any man on this subject, for did He not know all things and results I should not have known Christian Science, or felt the incipient touch of divine Love which inspired it.

That God is good, that Truth is true, and Science is Science, who can doubt; and whosoever demonstrates the truth of these propositions is to some extent a Christian Scientist. Is Science material? No! It is the Mind of God—and God is Spirit. Is Truth material? No!

Therefore I do not try to mix matter and Spirit, since Science does not and they will not mix. I am a spiritual homoeopathist in that I do not believe in such a compound. Truth and Truth is not a compound; Spirit and Spirit is not: but Truth and error, Spirit and matter, are compounds and opposites; so if one is true, the other is false. If Truth is true, its opposite, error, is not; and if Spirit is true and infinite, it hath no opposite; therefore matter cannot be a reality.

I begin at the feet of Christ and with the numeration table of Christian Science. But I do not say that one added to one is three, or one and a half, nor say this to accommodate popular opinion as to the Science of Christianity. I adhere to my text, that one and one are two all the way up to the infinite calculus of the infinite God. The numeration table of Christian Science, its divine Principle and rules, are before the people, and the different religious sects and the differing schools of medicine are discussing them as if they understood its Principle and rules before they have learned its numeration table, and insist that the public receive their sense of the Science, or that it receive no sense whatever of it.

Again: Even the numeration table of Christian Science is not taught correctly by those who have departed from its absolute simple statement as to Spirit and matter, and that one and two are neither more nor less than three; and losing the numeration table and the logic of Christian Science, they have little left that the sects and faculties can grapple. If Christian Scientists only would admit that God is Spirit and infinite, yet that God has an opposite and that the infinite is not all; that God is good and infinite, yet that evil exists and is real,—thence it would follow that evil must either exist in good, or exist outside of the *infinite*,—they would be in peace with the schools.

This departure, however, from the scientific statement, the divine Principle, rule, or demonstration of Christian Science, results as would a change of the denominations of mathematics; and you cannot demonstrate Christian Science except on its fixed Principle and given rule, according to the Master's teaching and proof. He was ultra; he was a reformer; he laid the axe at the root of all error, amalgamation, and compounds. He used no material medicine, nor recommended it, and taught his disciples and followers to do likewise; therefore he demonstrated his power over matter, sin, disease, and death, as no other person has ever demonstrated it.

Bishop Berkeley published a book in 1710 entitled "Treatise Concerning the Principle of Human Knowledge." Its object was to deny, on received principles of philosophy, the reality of an external material world. In later publications he declared physical substance to be "only the constant relation between phenomena connected by association and conjoined by the operations of the universal mind, nature being nothing more than conscious experience. Matter apart from conscious mind is an impossible and unreal concept." He denies the existence of matter, and argues that matter is not *without* the mind, but within it, and that that which is generally called matter is only an impression produced by divine power on the mind by means of invariable rules styled the laws of nature. Here he makes God the cause of all the ills of mortals and the casualties of earth.

Again, while descanting on the virtues of tar-water, he writes: "I esteem my having taken this medicine the greatest of all temporal blessings, and am convinced that under Providence I owe my life to it." Making matter more potent than Mind, when the storms of disease beat against Bishop Berkeley's metaphysics and personality he fell, and great was the fall—from divine metaphysics to tar-water !

Christian Science is more than two hundred years old. It dates beyond Socrates, Leibnitz, Berkeley, Darwin, or Huxley. It is as old as God, although its earthly advent is called the Christian era.

I had not read one line of Berkeley's writings when I published my work Science and Health, the Christian Science textbook.

In contradistinction to his views I found it necessary to follow Jesus' teachings, and none other, in order to demonstrate the divine Science of Christianity—the metaphysics of Christ—healing all manner of diseases. Philosophy, *materia medica*, and scholastic theology were inadequate to prove the doctrine of Jesus, and I relinquished the form to attain the spirit or mystery of godliness. Hence the mysticism, so called, of my writings becomes clear to the godly.

Building on the rock of Christ's teachings, we have a superstructure eternal in the heavens, omnipotent on earth, encompassing time and eternity. The stone which the builders reject is apt to be the cross, which they reject and whereby is won the crown and the head of the corner.

A knowledge of philosophy and of medicine, the scholasticism of a bishop, and the metaphysics (so called) which mix matter and mind,—certain individuals call aids to divine metaphysics, and regret their lack in my books, which because of their more spiritual import heal the sick ! No Christly axioms, practices, or parables are alluded to or required in such metaphysics, and the demonstration of matter minus, and God all, ends in some specious folly.

The great Metaphysician, Christ Jesus, denounced all such gilded sepulchres of his time and of all time. He never recommended drugs, he never used them. What, then, is our authority in Christianity for metaphysics based on materialism? He demonstrated what he taught. Had he taught the power of Spirit, and along with this the power of matter, he would have been as contradictory as the blending of good and evil, and the latter superior, which Satan demanded in the beginning, and which has since been avowed to be as real, and matter as useful, as the infinite God,—good,—which, if indeed Spirit and infinite, excludes evil and matter. Jesus likened such self-contradictions to a kingdom divided against itself, that cannot stand.

The unity and consistency of Jesus' theory and practice give my tired sense of false philosophy and material theology rest. The great teacher, preacher, and demonstrator of Christianity is the Master, who founded his system of metaphysics only on Christ, Truth, and supported it by his words and deeds.

The five personal senses can have only a finite sense of the infinite: therefore the metaphysician is sensual that combines matter with Spirit. In one sentence he declaims against matter, in the next he endows it with a life-giving quality not to be found in God! and turns away from Christ's purely spiritual means to the schools and matter for help in times of need.

I have passed through deep waters to preserve Christ's vesture unrent; then, when land is reached and the world aroused, shall the word popularity be pinned to the seamless robe, and they cast lots for it? God forbid! Let it be left to such as see God—to the pure in spirit, and the meek that inherit the earth; left to them of a sound faith and charity, the greatest of which is charity 21—spiritual love. St. Paul said: "Though I speak with the tongues of men and of angels, and have not charity, I am become as sounding brass, or a tinkling cymbal."

Before leaving this subject of the old metaphysicians, allow me to add I have read little of their writings. I was not drawn to them by a native or an acquired taste for what was problematic and self-contradictory. What I have given to the world on the subject of metaphysical healing or Christian Science is the result of my ownobservation, experience, and final discovery, quiteindependent of all other authors except the Bible.

My critic also writes: "The best contributions that have been made to the literature of Christian Science have been by Mrs. Eddy's followers. I look to see some

St. Paul arise among the Christian Scientists who will interpret their ideas and principles more clearly, and apply them more rationally to human needs."

My works are the first ever published on Christian Science, and nothing has since appeared that is correct on this subject the basis whereof cannot be traced to some of those works. The application of Christian Science is healing and reforming mankind. If any one as yet has healed hopeless cases, such as I have in one to three interviews with the patients, I shall rejoice in being informed thereof. Or if a modern St. Paul could start thirty years ago without a Christian Scientist on earth, and in this interval number one million, and an equal number of sick healed, also sinners reformed and the habits and appetites of mankind corrected, why was it not done? God is no respecter of persons.

I have put less of my own personality into Christian Science than others do in proportion, as I have taken out of its metaphysics all matter and left Christian Science as it is, purely spiritual, Christlike—the Mind of God and not of man—born of the Spirit and not matter. Professor Agassiz said: "Every great scientific truth goes through three stages. First, people say it conflicts with the Bible. Next, they say it has been discovered before. Lastly, they say they had always believed it." Having passed through the first two stages, Christian Science must be approaching the last stage of the great naturalist's prophecy.

It is only by praying, watching, and working for the kingdom of heaven within us and upon earth, that we enter the strait and narrow way, whereof our Master said, "and few there be that find it."

Of the ancient writers since the first century of the Christian era perhaps none lived a more devout Christian life up to his highest understanding than St. Augustine. Some of his writings have been translated into almost every Christian tongue, and are classed with the choicest memorials of devotion both in Catholic and Protestant oratories.

Sacred history shows that those who have followed exclusively Christ's teaching, have been scourged in the synagogues and persecuted from city to city. But this is no cause for not following it; and my only apology for trying to follow it is that I love Christ more than all the world, and my demonstration of Christian Science in healing has proven to me beyond a doubt that Christ, Truth, is indeed the way of salvation from all that worketh or maketh a lie. As Jesus said: "It is enough for the disciple that he be as his master." It is well to know that even Christ Jesus, who was not popular among the worldlings in his age, is not popular with them in this age; hence the inference that he who would be popular if he could, is not a student of Christ Jesus.

After a hard and successful career reformers usually are handsomely provided for. Has the thought come to Christian Scientists, Have we housed, fed, clothed, or visited a reformer for that purpose? Have we looked after or even known of his sore necessities ? Gifts he needs not. God has provided the means for him while he was providing ways and means for others. But mortals in the advancing stages of their careers need the watchful and tender care of those who want to help them. The aged reformer should not be left to the mercy of those who are not glad to sacrifice for him even as he has sacrificed for others all the best of his earthly years.

I say this not because reformers are not loved, but because well-meaning people sometimes are inapt or selfish in showing their love. They are like children that go out from the parents who nurtured them, toiled for them, and enabled them to be grand coworkers for mankind, children who forget their parents' increasing years and needs, and whenever they return to the old home go not to help mother but to recruit themselves. Or, if they attempt to help their parents, and adverse winds are blowing, this is no excuse for waiting till the wind shifts. They should remember that mother worked and won for them by facing the winds. All honor and success to those who honor their father and mother. The individual who loves most, does most, and sacrifices most for the reformer, is the individual who soonest will walk in his footsteps.

To aid my students in starting under a tithe of my own difficulties, I allowed them for several years fifty cents on every book of mine that they sold. "With this percentage," students wrote me, "quite quickly we have regained our tuition for the college course."

Christian Scientists are persecuted even as all other religious denominations have been, since ever the primitive Christians, "of whom the world was not worthy." We err in thinking the object of vital Christianity is only the bequeathing of itself to the coming centuries. The successive utterances of reformers are essential to its propagation. The magnitude of its meaning forbids head-long haste, and the consciousness which is most imbued struggles to articulate itself.

Christian Scientists are practically non-resistants; they are too occupied with doing good, observing the Golden Rule, to retaliate or to seek redress; they are not quacks, giving birth to nothing and death to all,—but they are leaders of a reform in religion and in medicine, and they have no craft that is in danger.

Even religion and therapeutics need regenerating. Philanthropists, and the higher class of critics in theology and *materia medica*, recognize that Christian Science kindles the inner genial life of a man, destroying all lower considerations. No man or woman is roused to the estab-lishment of a new-old religion by the hope of ease, pleasure, or recompense, or by the stress of the appetites and pas-sions. And no emperor is obeyed like the man "clouting his own cloak"—working alone with God, yea, like the clear, far-seeing vision, the calm courage, and the great heart of the unselfed Christian hero.

I counsel Christian Scientists under all circumstances to obey the Golden Rule, and to adopt Pope's axiom: "An honest, sensible, and well-bred man will not insult me, and no other can." The sensualist and world-worshipper are always stung by a clear elucidation of truth, of right, and of wrong.

The only opposing element that sects or professions can encounter in Christian Science is Truth opposed to all error, specific or universal. This opposition springs from the very nature of Truth, being neither personal nor human, but divine. Every true Christian in the near future will learn and love the truths of Christian Science that now seem troublesome. Jesus said, "I came not to send peace but a sword."

Has God entrusted me with a message to mankind?— then I cannot choose but obey. After a long acquaintance with the communicants of my large church, they regard me with no vague, fruitless, inquiring wonder. I can use the power that God gives me in no way except in the interest of the individual and the community. To this verity every member of my church would bear loving testimony.

MY CHILDHOOD'S CHURCH HOME

Among the list of blessings infinite I count these dear: Devout orthodox parents; my early culture in the Congregational Church; the daily Bible reading and family prayer; my cradle hymn and the Lord's Prayer, repeated at night; my early association with distinguished Christian clergymen, who held fast to whatever is good, used faithfully God's Word, and yielded up graciously what He took away. It was my fair fortune to be often taught by some grand old divines, among whom were the Rev.

Abraham Burnham of Pembroke, N. H., Rev. Nathaniel Bouton, D. D., of Concord, N. H., Congregationalists; Rev. Mr. Boswell, of Bow, N. H., Baptist; Rev. Enoch Corser, and Rev. Corban Curtice, Congregationalists; and Father Hinds, Methodist Elder. I became early a child of the Church, an eager lover and student of vital Christianity. Why I loved Christians of the old sort was I could not help loving them. Full of charity and good works, busy about their Master's business, they had no time or desire to defame their fellow-men. God seemed to shield the whole world in their hearts, and they were willing to renounce all for Him. When infidels assailed them, however, the courage of their convictions was seen. They were heroes in the strife; they armed quickly, aimed deadly, and spared no denunciation. Their convictions were honest, and they lived them; and the sermons their lives preached caused me to love their doctrines.

The lives of those old-fashioned leaders of religion explain in a few words a good man. They fill the ecclesiastic measure, that to love God and keep His commandments is the whole duty of man. Such churchmen and the Bible, especially the First Commandment of the Decalogue, and Ninety-first Psalm, the Sermon on the Mount, and St. John's Revelation, educated my thought many years, yea, all the way up to its preparation for and reception of the Science of Christianity. I believe, if those venerable Christians were here to-day, their sanctified souls would take in the spirit and understanding of Christian Science through the flood-gates of Love; with them Love was the governing impulse of every action; their piety was the all-important consideration of their being, the original beauty of holiness that to-day seems to be fading so sensibly from our sight.

To plant for eternity, the "accuser" or "calumniator" must not be admitted to the vineyard of our Lord, and the hand of love must sow the seed. Carlyle writes: "Quackery and dupery do abound in religion; above all, in the more advanced decaying stages of religion, they have fearfully abounded; but quackery was never the originating influence in such things; it was not the health and life of religion, but their disease, the sure precursor that they were about to die."

Christian Scientists first and last ask not to be judged on a doctrinal platform, a creed, or a diploma for scientific guessing. But they do ask to be allowed the rights of conscience and the protection of the constitutional laws of their land; they ask to be known by their works, to be judged (if at all) by their works. We admit that they do not kill people with poisonous drugs, with the lance, or with liquor, in order to heal them. Is it for not killing them thus, or is it for healing them through the might and majesty of divine power after the manner taught by Jesus, and which he enjoined his students to teach and practise, that they are maligned? The richest and most positive proof that a religion in this century is just what it was in the first centuries is that the same reviling it received then it receives now, and from the same motives which actuate one sect to persecute another in advance of it.

Christian Scientists are harmless citizens that do not kill people either by their practice or by preventing the early employment of an M.D. Why? Because the effect of prayer, whereby Christendom saves sinners, is quite as salutary in the healing of all manner of diseases. The Bible is our authority for asserting this, in both cases. The interval that detains the patient from the attendance of an M.D., occupied in prayer and in spiritual obedience to Christ's mode and means of healing, cannot be fatal to the patient, and is proven to be more pathological than the M.D.'s material prescription. If this be not so, where shall we look for the standard of Christianity? Have we misread the evangelical precepts and the canonical writings of the Fathers, or must we have a new Bible and a new system of Christianity, originating not in God, but a creation of the schools—a material religion, proscriptive, intolerant, wantonly bereft of the Word of God.

Give us, dear God, again on earth the lost chord of Christ; solace us with the song of angels rejoicing with them that rejoice; that sweet charity which seeketh not her own but another's good, yea, which *knoweth no evil*.

Finally, brethren, wait patiently on God; return blessing for cursing; be not overcome of evil, but overcome evil with good; be steadfast, abide and abound in faith, understanding, and good works; study the Bible and the textbook of our denomination; obey strictly the laws that be, and follow your Leader only so far as she follows Christ. Godliness or Christianity is a human necessity: man cannot live without it; he has no intelligence, health, hope, nor happiness without godliness. In the words of the Hebrew writers: "Trust in the Lord with all thine heart; and lean not unto thine own understanding. In all thy ways acknowledge Him, and He shall direct thy paths;" "and He shall bring forth thy righteousness as the light, and thy judgment as the noonday."

The question oft presents itself, Are we willing to sacrifice self for the Cause of Christ, willing to bare our bosom to the blade and lay ourselves upon the altar? Christian Science appeals loudly to those asleep upon the hill-tops of Zion. It is a clarion call to the reign of righteousness, to the kingdom of heaven within us and on earth, and Love is the way alway.

O the Love divine that plucks us
From the human agony!
O the Master's glory won thus,
Doth it dawn on you and me?
And the bliss of blotted-out sin
And the working hitherto—
Shall we share it—do we walk in
Patient faith the way thereto?

APPENDIX

TENETS OF THE MOTHER CHURCH
THE FIRST CHURCH OF CHRIST, SCIENTIST

To be signed by those uniting with The First Church of Christ, Scientist, in Boston, Mass.

1. As adherents of Truth, we take the inspired Word of the Bible as our sufficient guide to eternal Life.

2. We acknowledge and adore one supreme and infinite God. We acknowledge His Son, one Christ; the Holy Ghost or divine Comforter; and man in God's image and likeness.

3. We acknowledge God's forgiveness of sin in the destruction of sin and the spiritual understanding that casts out evil as unreal. But the belief in sin is punished so long as the belief lasts.

4. We acknowledge Jesus's atonement as the evidence of divine, efficacious Love, unfolding man's unity with God through Christ Jesus the Way-shower; and we acknowledge that man is saved through Christ, through Truth, Life, and Love as demonstrated by the Galilean Prophet in healing the sick and overcoming sin and death.

5. We acknowledge that the crucifixion of Jesus and his resurrection served to uplift the faith to understand eternal Life, even the allness of Soul, Spirit, and the nothingness of matter.

6. And we solemnly promise to watch, and pray for that Mind to be in us which was also in Christ Jesus; to do unto others as we would have them do unto us; and to be merciful, just, and pure.

CHRISTIAN HEALING
SERMON DELIVERED AT BOSTON, 1886

TEXT: *And these signs shall follow them that believe; In my name shall they cast out devils; they shall speak with new tongues; they shall take up serpents; and if they drink any deadly thing, it shall not hurt them; they shall lay hands on the sick, and they shall recover.*

—MARK xvi. 17, 18

HISTORY repeats itself; to-morrow grows out of to-day. But Heaven's favors are formidable: they are calls to higher duties, not discharge from care; and whoso builds on less than an immortal basis, hath built on sand.

We have asked, in our selfishness, to wait until the age advanced to a more practical and spiritual religion before arguing with the world the great subject of Christian heal-ing; but our answer was, "Then there were no cross to take up, and less need of publishing the good news." A classic writes,—

> "At thirty, man suspects himself a fool;
> Knows it at forty, and reforms his plan;
> At fifty, chides his infamous delay,
> Pushes his prudent purpose to resolve."

The difference between religions is, that one religion has a more spiritual basis and tendency than the other; and the religion nearest right is that one. The genius of Christianity is works more than words; a calm and stead-fast communion with God; a tumult on earth,—religious factions and prejudices arrayed against it, the synagogues as of old closed upon it, while it reasons with the storm, hurls the thunderbolt of truth, and stills the tempest of error; scourged and condemned at every advancing footstep, afterwards pardoned and adopted, but never seen amid the smoke of battle. Said the intrepid reformer, Martin Luther: "I am weary of the world, and the world is weary of me; the parting will be easy." Said the more gentle Melanchthon: "Old Adam is too strong for young Melanchthon."

And still another Christian hero, ere he passed from his execution to a crown, added his testimony: "I have fought a good fight, . . . I have kept the faith." But Jesus, the model of infinite patience, said: "Come unto me, all ye that labor and are heavy laden, and I will give you rest." And he said this when bending beneath the malice of the world. But why should the world hate Jesus, the loved of the Father, the loved of Love? It was that his spirituality rebuked their carnality, and gave this proof of Christianity that religions had not given. Again, they knew it was not in the power of eloquence or a dead rite to cast out error and heal the sick. Past, present, future magnifies his name who built, on Truth, eternity's foundation stone, and sprinkled the altar of Love with perpetual incense.

Such Christianity requires neither hygiene nor drugs wherewith to heal both mind and body; or, lacking these, to show its helplessness. The primitive privilege of Christianity was to make men better, to cast out error, and heal the sick. It was a proof, more than a profession thereof; a demonstration, more than a doctrine. It was the foundation of right thinking and right acting, and must be reestablished on its former basis. The stone which the

builders rejected must again become the head of the
corner. In proportion as the personal and material element stole into religion, it lost Christianity and the power
to heal; and the qualities of God as a person, instead of
the divine Principle that begets the quality, engrossed the
attention of the ages. In the original text the term *God*
was derived from the word *good.* Christ is the idea
of Truth; Jesus is the name of a man born in a remote
province of Judea,—Josephus alludes to several individuals by the name of Jesus. Therefore Christ Jesus was
an honorary title; it signified a "good man," which epithet the great goodness and wonderful works of our
Master more than merited. Because God is the Principle of
Christian healing, we must understand in part this divine
Principle, or we cannot demonstrate it in part.

The Scriptures declare that "God is Love, Truth, and
Life,"—a trinity in unity; not three persons in one, but
three statements of one Principle. We cannot tell what is
the person of Truth, the body of the infinite, but we know
that the Principle is not the person, that the finite cannot
contain the infinite, that unlimited Mind cannot start from
a limited body. The infinite can neither go forth from,
return to, nor remain for a moment within limits. We
must give freer breath to thought before calculating the
results of an infinite Principle,—the effects of infinite
Love, the compass of infinite Life, the power of infinite
Truth. Clothing Deity with personality, we limit the action of God to the finite senses. We pray for God to remember us, even as we ask a person with softening of the
brain not to forget his daily cares. We ask infinite wisdom
to possess our finite sense, and forgive what He knows
deserves to be punished, and to bless what is unfit to be

APPENDIX

blessed. We expect infinite Love to drop divinity long
enough to hate. We expect infinite Truth to mix with
error, and become finite for a season; and, after infinite
Spirit is forced in and out of matter for an indefinite period,
to show itself infinite again. We expect infinite Life to
become finite, and have an end; but, after a temporary
lapse, to begin anew as infinite Life, without beginning and
without end.

Friends, can we ever arrive at a proper conception of the
divine character, and gain a right idea of the Principle of
all that is right, with such self-evident contradictions?
God must be our model, or we have none; and if this
model is one thing at one time, and the opposite of it at
another, can we rely on our model? Or, having faith in it,
how can we demonstrate a changing Principle? We cannot: we shall be consistent with our inconsistent statement
of Deity, and so bring out our own erring finite sense of
God, and of good and evil blending. While admitting
that God is omnipotent, we shall be limiting His power at
every point,—shall be saying He is beaten by certain kinds
of food, by changes of temperature, the neglect of a bath,
and so on. Phrenology will be saying the developments of
the brain bias a man's character. Physiology will be saying, if a man has taken cold by doing good to his neighbor,
God will punish him now for the cold, but he must wait for
the reward of his good deed hereafter. One of our leading clergymen startles us by saying that "between Christianity and spiritualism, the question chiefly is concerning
the trustworthiness of the communications, and not the
doubt of their reality." Does any one think the departed
are not departed, but are with us, although we have no
evidence of the fact except sleight-of-hand and hallu-
cination?

Such hypotheses ignore Biblical authority, obscure the one grand truth which is constantly covered, in one way or another, from our sight. This truth is, that we are to work out our own salvation, and to meet the responsibility of our own thoughts and acts; relying not on the person of God or the person of man to do our work for us, but on the apostle's rule, "I will show thee my faith by my works." This spiritualism would lead our lives to higher issues; it would purify, elevate, and consecrate man; it would teach him that "whatsoever a man soweth, that shall he also reap." The more spiritual we become here, the more are we separated from the world; and should this rule fail hereafter, and we grow more material, and so come back to the world? When I was told the other day, "People say you are a medium," pardon me if I smiled. The pioneer of something new under the sun is never hit: he cannot be; the opinions of people fly too high or too low. From my earliest investigations of the mental phenomenon named mediumship, I knew it was misinterpreted, and I said it. The spiritualists abused me for it then, and have ever since; but they take pleasure in calling me a medium. I saw the impossibility, in Science, of intercommunion between the so-called dead and the living. When I learned how mind produces disease on the body, I learned how it produces the manifestations ignorantly imputed to spirits. I saw how the mind's ideals were evolved and made tangible; and it matters not whether that ideal is a flower or a cancer, if the belief is strong enough to manifest it. Man thinks he is a medium of disease; that when he is sick, disease controls his body to whatever manifestation we see. But the fact remains, in metaphysics, that the mind of the individual only can produce a result upon his body. The belief that produces this result may be wholly unknown to the individual, because it is lying back in the unconscious thought, a latent cause producing the effect we see.

"And these signs shall follow them that believe; In my name shall they cast out devils." The word *devil* comes from the Greek *diabolos*; in Hebrew it is *belial*, and signifies "that which is good for nothing, lust," etc. The signs referred to are the manifestations of the power of Truth to cast out error; and, correcting error in thought, it produces the harmonious effect on the body. "Them that believe" signifies those who understand God's supremacy,—the power of Mind over matter. "The new tongue" is the spiritual meaning as opposed to the material. It is the language of Soul instead of the senses; it translates matter into its original language, which is Mind, and gives the spiritual instead of the material signification. It begins with motive, instead of act, where Jesus formed his estimate; and there correcting the motive, it corrects the act that results from the motive. The Science of Christianity makes pure the fountain, in order to purify the stream. It begins in mind to heal the body, the same as it begins in motive to correct the act, and through which to judge of it. The Master of metaphysics, reading the mind of the poor woman who dropped her mite into the treasury, said, "She hath cast in more than they all." Again, he charged home a crime to mind, regardless of any outward act, and sentenced it as our judges would not have done to-day. Jesus knew that adultery is a crime, and *mind* is the criminal. I wish the age was up to his understanding of these two facts, so important to progress and Christianity.

"They shall take up serpents; and if they drink any deadly thing, it shall not hurt them. " This is an unqualified

statement of the duty and ability of Christians to heal
the sick; and it contains no argument for a creed or doctrine, it implies no necessity beyond the understanding of
God, and obedience to His government, that heals both
mind and body; God,—not a person to whom we should
pray to heal the sick, but the Life, Love, and Truth that
destroy error and death. Understanding the truth regarding mind and body, knowing that Mind can master sickness as well as sin, and carrying out this government over
both and bringing out the results of this higher Christianity, we shall perceive the meaning of the context,
—"They shall lay hands on the sick, and they shall
recover."

The world is slow to perceive individual advancement;
but when it reaches the thought that has produced this,
then it is willing to be made whole, and no longer quarrels
with the individual. Plato did better; he said, "What
thou seest, that thou beest."

The mistaken views entertained of Deity becloud the
light of revelation, and suffocate reason by materialism.
When we understand that God is what the Scriptures have
declared,—namely, Life, Truth, and Love,—we shall
learn to reach heaven through Principle instead of a pardon; and this will make us honest and laborious, knowing
that we shall receive only what we have earned. Jesus
illustrated this by the parable of the husbandman. If we
work to become Christians as honestly and as directly
upon a divine Principle, and adhere to the rule of this
Principle as directly as we do to the rule of mathematics,
we shall be Christian Scientists, and do more than we
are now doing, and progress faster than we are now

pro gressing. We should have no anxiety about what is
or what is not the person of God, if we understood the
Principle better and employed our thoughts more in demonstrating it. We are constantly thinking and talking
on the wrong side of the question. The less said or thought
of sin, sickness, or death, the better for mankind, morally
and physically. The greatest sinner and the most hopeless invalid think most of sickness and of sin; but, having
learned that this method has not saved them from either,
why do they go on thus, and their moral advisers talk for
them on the very subjects they would gladly discontinue to
bring out in their lives? Contending for the reality of
what should disappear is like furnishing fuel for the flames.
Is it a duty for any one to believe that "the curse causeless
cannot come"? Then it is a higher duty to know that
God never cursed man, His own image and likeness. God
never made a wicked man; and man made by God had not
a faculty or power underived from his Maker wherewith to
make himself wicked.

The only correct answer to the question, "Who is
the author of evil?" is the scientific statement that
evil is unreal; that God made all that was made, but
He never made sin or sickness, either an error of mind
or of body. Life in matter is a dream: sin, sickness,
and death are this dream. Life is Spirit; and when we
waken from the dream of life in matter, we shall learn this
grand truth of being. St. John saw the vision of life in
matter; and he saw it pass away,—an illusion. The
dragon that was wroth with the woman, and stood ready
"to devour the child as soon as it was born," was the vision
of envy, sensuality, and malice, ready to devour the idea
of Truth. But the beast bowed before the Lamb: it was

supposed to have fought the manhood of God, that Jesus represented; but it fell before the womanhood of God, that presented the highest ideal of Love. Let us remember that God—good—is omnipotent; therefore evil is impotent. There is but one side to good,—it has no evil side; there is but one side to reality, and that is the good side.

God is All, and in all: that finishes the question of a good and a bad side to existence. Truth is the real; error is the unreal. You will gather the importance of this saying, when sorrow seems to come, if you will look on the bright side; for sorrow endureth but for the night, and joy cometh with the light. Then will your sorrow be a dream, and your waking the reality, even the triumph of Soul over sense. If you wish to be happy, argue with yourself on the side of happiness; take the side you wish to carry, and be careful not to talk on both sides, or to argue stronger for sorrow than for joy. You are the attorney for the case, and will win or lose according to your plea.

As the mountain hart panteth for the water brooks, so panteth my heart for the true fount and Soul's baptism. Earth's fading dreams are empty streams, her fountains play in borrowed sunbeams, her plumes are plucked from the wings of vanity. Did we survey the cost of sublunary joy, we then should gladly waken to see it was unreal. A dream calleth itself a dreamer, but when the dream has passed, man is seen wholly apart from the dream.

We are in the midst of a revolution; physics are yielding slowly to metaphysics; mortal mind rebels at its own boundaries; weary of matter, it would catch the meaning of Spirit. The only immortal superstructure is built on Truth; her modest tower rises slowly, but it stands and is the miracle of the hour, though it may seem to the age like the great pyramid of Egypt,—a miracle in stone. The fires of ancient proscription burn upon the altars of to-day; he who has suffered from intolerance is the first to be intolerant. Homoeopathy may not recover from the heel of allopathy before lifting its foot against its neighbor, metaphysics, although homoeopathy has laid the foundation stone of mental healing; it has established this axiom, "The less medicine the better," and metaphysics adds, "until you arrive at no medicine." When you have reached this high goal you have learned that proportionately as matter went out and Mind came in as the remedy, was its potency. Metaphysics places all cause and cure as mind; differing in this from homoeopathy, where cause and cure are supposed to be both mind and matter. Metaphysics requires mind imbued with Truth to heal the sick; hence the Christianity of metaphysical healing, and this excellence above other systems. The higher attenuations of homoeopathy contain no medicinal properties, and thus it is found out that Mind instead of matter heals the sick.

While the matter-physician feels the pulse, examines the tongue, etc., to learn what matter is doing independent of mind, when it is self-evident it can do nothing, the metaphysician goes to the fount to govern the streams; he diagnoses disease as mind, the basis of all action, and cures it thus when matter cannot cure it, showing he was right. Thus it was we discovered that all physical effects originate in mind before they can become manifest as matter; we learned from the Scripture and Christ's healing that God, directly or indirectly, through His providence or His laws, never made a man sick. When studying the two hundred and sixty remedies of the Jahr, the characteristic peculiarities and the general and moral symptoms requiring the remedy, we saw at once the concentrated power of thought brought to bear on the pharmacy of homoeopathy, which made the infinitesimal dose effectual. To prepare the medicine requires time and thought; you cannot shake the poor drug without the involuntary thought, "I am making you more powerful," and the sequel proves it; the higher attenuations prove that the power was the thought, for when the drug disappears by your process the power remains, and homoeopathists admit the higher attenuations are the most powerful. The only objection to giving the unmedicated sugar is, it would be dishonest and divide one's faith apparently between matter and mind, and so weaken both points of action; taking hold of both horns of the dilemma, we should work at opposites and accomplish less on either side.

The pharmacy of homoeopathy is reducing the one hundredth part of a grain of medicine two thousand times, shaking the preparation thirty times at every attenuation. There is a moral to this medicine; the higher natures are reached soonest by the higher attenuations, until the fact is found out they have taken no medicine, and then the so-called drug loses its power. We have attenuated a grain of aconite until it was no longer aconite, then dropped into a tumblerful of water a single drop of this harmless solution, and administering one teaspoonful of this water at intervals of half an hour have cured the incipient stage of fever. The highest attenuation we ever attained was to leave the drug out of the question, using only the sugar of milk; and with this original dose we cured an inveterate case of dropsy. After these experiments you cannot be surprised that we resigned the imaginary medicine altogether, and honestly employed Mind as the only curative Principle.

What are the foundations of metaphysical healing? *Mind*, divine Science, the truth of being that casts out error and thus heals the sick. You can readily perceive this mental system of healing is the antipode of mesmerism, Beelzebub. Mesmerism makes one disease while it is supposed to cure another, and that one is worse than the first; mesmerism is one lie getting the better of another, and the bigger lie occupying the field for a period; it is the fight of beasts, in which the bigger animal beats the lesser; in fine, much ado about nothing. Medicine will not arrive at the science of treating disease until disease is treated mentally and man is healed morally and physically. What has physiology, hygiene, or physics done for Christianity but to obscure the divine Principle of healing and encourage faith in an opposite direction?

Great caution should be exercised in the choice of physicians. If you employ a medical practitioner, be sure he is a learned man and skilful; never trust yourself in the hands of a quack. In proportion as a physician is enlightened and liberal is he equipped with Truth, and his efforts are salutary; ignorance and charlatanism are miserable medical aids. Metaphysical healing includes infinitely more than merely to know that mind governs the body and the method of a mental practice. The preparation for a metaphysical practitioner is the most arduous task I ever performed. You must first mentally educate and develop the spiritual sense or perceptive faculty by which one learns the metaphysical treatment of disease; you must teach them how to learn, together with what they learn. I waited many years for a student to reach the ability to teach; it included more than they understood.

Metaphysical or divine Science reveals the Principle and method of perfection,—how to attain a mind in harmony with God, in sympathy with all that is right and opposed to all that is wrong, and a body governed by this mind.

Christian Science repudiates the evidences of the senses and rests upon the supremacy of God. Christian healing, established upon this Principle, vindicates the omnipotence of the Supreme Being by employing no other remedy than Truth, Life, and Love, understood, to heal all ills that flesh is heir to. It places no faith in hygiene or drugs; it reposes all faith in mind, in spiritual power divinely directed. By rightly understanding the power of mind over matter, it enables mind to govern matter, as it rises to that supreme sense that shall "take up serpents" unharmed, and "if they drink any deadly thing, it shall not hurt them. " Christian Science explains to any one's perfect satisfaction the so-called miracles recorded in the Bible. Ah! why should man deny all might to the divine Mind, and claim another mind perpetually at war with this Mind, when at the same time he calls God almighty and admits in statement what he denies in proof? You pray for God to heal you, but should you expect this when you are acting oppositely to your prayer, trying everything else besides God, and believe that sickness is something He cannot reach, but medicine can? as if drugs were superior to Deity.

The Scripture says, "Ye ask, and receive not, because
ye ask amiss;" and is it not asking amiss to pray for a
proof of divine power, that you have little or no faith in
because you do not understand God, the Principle of
this proof? Prayer will be inaudible, and works more
than words, as we understand God better. The Lord's
Prayer, understood in its spiritual sense, and given its
spiritual version, can never be repeated too often for the
benefit of all who, having ears, hear and understand.
Metaphysical Science teaches us there is no other Life,
substance, and intelligence but God. How much are you
demonstrating of this statement? which to you hath the
most actual substance,—wealth and fame, or Truth and
Love? See to it, O Christian Scientists, ye who have
named the name of Christ with a higher meaning, that you
abide by your statements, and abound in Love and Truth,
for unless you do this you are not demonstrating the
Science of metaphysical healing. The immeasurable
Life and Love will occupy your affections, come nearer
your hearts and into your homes when you touch but the
hem of Truth's garment.

A word about the five personal senses, and we will leave
our abstract subjects for this time. The only evidence we
have of sin, sickness, or death is furnished by these senses;
but how can we rely on their testimony when the senses
afford no evidence of Truth? They can neither see, hear,
feel, taste, nor smell God; and shall we call that reliable
evidence through which we can gain no understanding of
Truth, Life, and Love? Again, shall we say that God
hath created those senses through which it is impossible to
approach Him? Friends, it is of the utmost importance
that we look into these subjects, and gain our evidences of
Life from the correct source. Jesus said, "I am the way,

the truth, and the life. No man cometh unto the Father, but by me,"—through the footsteps of Truth. Not by the senses—the lusts of the flesh, the pride of life, envy, hypocrisy, or malice, the pleasures or the pains of the personal senses—does man get nearer his divine nature and present the image and likeness of God. How, then, can it be that material man and the personal senses were created by God? Love makes the spiritual man, lust makes the material so-called man, and God made all that was made; therefore the so-called material man and these personal senses, with all their evidences of sin, sickness, and death, are but a dream,—they are not the realities of life; and we shall all learn this as we awake to behold His likeness.

The allegory of Adam, when spiritually understood, explains this dream of material life, even the dream of the "deep sleep" that fell upon Adam when the spiritual senses were hushed by material sense that before had claimed audience with a serpent. Sin, sickness, and death never proceeded from Truth, Life, and Love. Sin, sickness, and death are error; they are not Truth, and therefore are not TRUE. Sin is a supposed mental condition; sickness and death are supposed physical ones, but all appeared through the false supposition of life and intelligence in matter. Sin was first in the allegory, and sickness and death were produced by sin. Then was not sin of mental origin, and did not mind originate the delusion? If sickness and death came through mind, so must they go; and are we not right in ruling them out of mind to destroy their effects upon the body, that both mortal mind and mortal body shall yield to the government of God, immortal Mind? In the words of Paul, that "the old man" shall be "put off," mortality shall

disappear and immortality be brought to light. People are
willing to put new wine into old bottles; but if this be
done, the bottle will break and the wine be spilled.

There is no connection between Spirit and matter.
Spirit never entered and it never escaped from matter;
good and evil never dwelt together. There is in reality
but the good: Truth is the real; error, the unreal. We
cannot put the new wine into old bottles. If that could be
done, the world would accept our sentiments; it would willingly adopt the new idea, if that idea could be reconciled
with the old belief; it would put the new wine into the
old bottle if it could prevent its effervescing and keep it
from popping out until it became popular.

The doctrine of atonement never did anything for sickness or claimed to reach that woe; but Jesus' mission
extended to the sick as much as to the sinner: he established his Messiahship on the basis that Christ, Truth,
heals the sick. Pride, appetites, passions, envy, and malice
will cease to assert their Caesar sway when metaphysics is
understood; and religion at the sick-bed will be no blind
Samson shorn of his locks. You must admit that what is
termed death has been produced by a belief alone. The
Oxford students proved this: they killed a man by no other
means than making him believe he was bleeding to death.
A felon was delivered to them for experiment to test the
power of mind over body; and they did test it, and proved
it. They proved it not in part, but as a whole; they
proved that every organ of the system, every function of
the body, is governed directly and entirely by mind, else
those functions could not have been stopped by mind in-
dependently of material conditions. Had they changed
the felon's belief that he was bleeding to death, removed

the bandage from his eyes, and he had seen that a vein had not been opened, he would have resuscitated. The illusive origin of disease is not an exception to the origin of all mortal things. Spirit is causation, and the ancient question, Which is first, the egg or the bird? is answered by the Scripture, He made "every plant of the field before it was in the earth."

Heaven's signet is Love. We need it to stamp our religions and to spiritualize thought, motive, and endeavor. Tireless Being, patient of man's procrastination, affords him fresh opportunities every hour; but if Science makes a more spiritual demand, bidding man go up higher, he is impatient perhaps, or doubts the feasibility of the demand. But let us work more earnestly in His vineyard, and according to the model on the mount, bearing the cross meekly along the rugged way, into the wilderness, up the steep ascent, on to heaven, making our words golden rays in the sunlight of our deeds; and "these signs shall follow them that believe; . . . they shall lay hands on the sick, and they shall recover."

The following hymn was sung at the close:—

"Oh, could we speak the matchless worth,
Oh, could we sound the glories forth,
Which in our Saviour shine,
We'd soar and touch the heavenly strings,
And vie with Gabriel, while he sings,
*   In notes almost divine."*

1821 **July 16:** Mary Morse Baker is born in Bow, New Hampshire; she is the last of six children of Mark and Abigail Ambrose Baker

1836 **January:** Bakers move to a new farm near Sanbornton Bridge (now Tilton), New Hampshire

1841 Albert Baker dies of kidney disease

1843 **December 10:** Mary Baker marries George Washington Glover

1844 **June 27:** George Glover dies of yellow fever, leaving Mary pregnant and penniless

September 12: Mary gives birth to her first and only child, George Washington Glover, Jr.

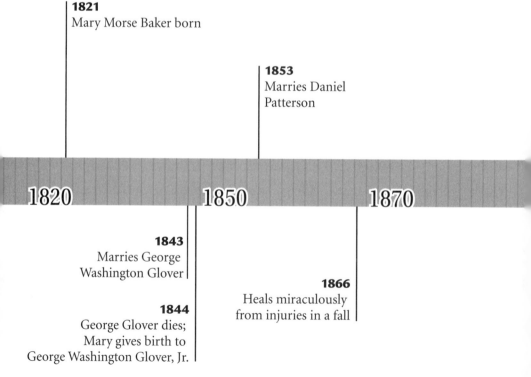

1821
Mary Morse Baker born

1853
Marries Daniel
Patterson

1820　1850　1870

1843
Marries George
Washington Glover

1844
George Glover dies;
Mary gives birth to
George Washington Glover, Jr.

1866
Heals miraculously
from injuries in a fall

1849   **November 12:** Mother, Abigail Ambrose Baker, dies

1850   **December:** Mark Baker marries Elizabeth Patterson Duncan

1851   **May:** Son, George, is sent to live in North Groton, New Hampshire, with Mahala and Russell Cheney

1853   **June 21:** Mary weds Daniel Patterson, dentist and homoeopathist

1862   **October:** Mary receives treatment from Phineas P. Quimby in Portland, Maine

1866   Mary is seriously injured in a fall on ice; she is miraculously healed at home in Swampscott, Massachusetts

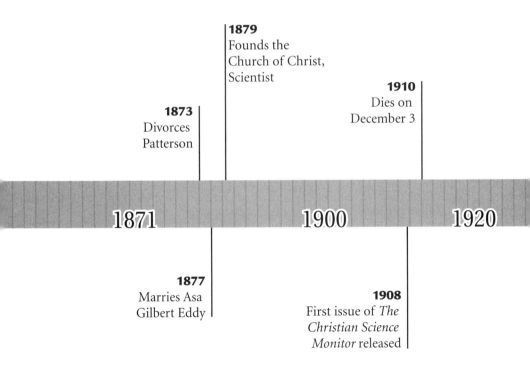

1879
Founds the
Church of Christ,
Scientist

1910
Dies on
December 3

1873
Divorces
Patterson

1871   **1900**   **1920**

1877
Marries Asa
Gilbert Eddy

1908
First issue of *The
Christian Science
Monitor* released

1866–1868 Mary moves from house to house; works on her writings

1873 Mary divorces Patterson

1875 Mary buys a house at 8 Broad Street, Lynn, Massachusetts; publishes *Science and Health*

1876 Organizes the Christian Scientist Association

1877 Marries Asa Gilbert Eddy

1878 **October 29:** Edward Arens and Gilbert Eddy are arrested on suspicion of conspiring to murder Daniel Spofford

1879 Founds the Church of Christ, Scientist

1881 The Massachusetts Metaphysical College is chartered

1882 Gilbert Eddy dies

1883 The first issue of *The Journal of Christian Science* is published

1888 Mary delivers her moving speech at Central Music Hall in Chicago

1889 Mary closes the Massachusetts Metaphysical College and moves to Concord, New Hampshire; the church is formally disorganized

1891 Publishes a major revision (the fifty-second) of *Science and Health With Key to the Scriptures*

1892 Mary moves to Pleasant View, New Hampshire; the Mother Church is formally reorganized

1895 The Mother Church is dedicated; Mary does not attend the ceremony

1898 Mary teaches her last class in Concord

1899 Frederick Peabody files a suit against Mary and church officials on behalf of Josephine Woodbury; the case later collapses in court (June 1901)

1907 William Chandler and George Glover begin the Next Friends suit; Mary wins the case

1908 Mary moves to Chestnut Hill, Massachusetts; the first issue of *The Christian Science Monitor* appears

1910 **December 3:** Mary dies at home in Chestnut Hill, probably of pneumonia

NOTES

CHAPTER 1: A Great Discovery

1 Robert Peel, *Mary Baker Eddy: The Years of Discovery*, New York: Holt Rinehart and Winston, 1977, p. 196.

2 Ibid.; this account was recalled by Arietta Brown, daughter of Mary's friend, Mrs. Ira Brown, who was nine years old at the time of the incident.

3 Mary Baker Eddy, *Retrospection and Introspection*, Boston: The First Church of Christ, Scientist, 1920, p. 24.

4 Peel, p. 197.

CHAPTER 2: Growing up

5 Samuel Dow was born on July 8, 1808; Albert on February 5, 1810; George Sullivan on August 7, 1812; Abigail Barnard on January 15, 1816; and Martha Smith on January 19, 1819. The children were given common names of the era. To distinguish their children from others, the Bakers gave them each a middle name chosen to honor a close friend or relative.

6 Robert Peel, *Mary Baker Eddy: The Years of Discovery*, New York: Holt Rinehart and Winston, 1977, p. 31.

7 Mary Baker Eddy, *Retrospection and Introspection*, Boston: The First Church of Christ, Scientist, 1920, p. 6.

8 Ibid., pp. 5–6; this reference is taken from the eulogy given by the Reverend Richard S. Rust at Abigail Baker's funeral.

9 Ibid., p. 6.

10 Peel, p. 23.

11 Louise A. Smith, *Mary Baker Eddy: Discoverer and Founder of Christian Science*, Boston: Christian Science Publishing Society, 1991, p. 17.

12 Peel, p. 24.

13 Ibid.

14 Ibid.

15 Smith, p. 18.

16 Ibid.

17 Ibid., p. 19.

18 Ibid., p. 10.

19 Eddy, *Retrospection and Introspection*, pp. 8–9.

20 Gillian Gill, *Mary Baker Eddy*, Cambridge, MA: Perseus Books, 1999, p. 13.

21 Eddy, *Retrospection and Introspection*, p. 13.

22 Ibid., pp. 13–14.

23 Ibid., p. 14.

CHAPTER 3: To Sanbornton Bridge

24 Louise A. Smith, *Mary Baker Eddy: Discoverer and Founder of Christian Science*, Boston: Christian Science Publishing Society, 1991, p. 24.

25 Robert Peel, *Mary Baker Eddy: The Years of Discovery*, New York: Holt Rinehart and Winston, 1977, p. 26.

26 Ibid., p. 27.

27 Ibid., p. 38.

28 Ibid.

29 Ibid., p. 42.

30 Smith, p. 28.

31 Mary Baker Eddy, *Retrospection and Introspection*, Boston: The First Church of Christ, Scientist, 1920, p. 6.

32 Gillian Gill, *Mary Baker Eddy*, Cambridge, MA: Perseus Books, 1999, p. 19.

33 Peel, p. 62.

34 Ibid., p. 63.

35 Smith, p. 32.

36 Ibid., p. 34.

37 Ibid., p. 35.

38 Peel, p. 69.

39 Ibid., p. 76.

CHAPTER 4: Years of Trial

40 Later in life, Mary often compared her relationship to the church with that between a mother and child. See Robert Peel, *Mary Baker Eddy: The Years of Discovery*, New York: Holt Rinehart and Winston, 1977, p. 79.

41 Louise A. Smith, *Mary Baker Eddy: Discoverer and Founder of Christian Science*, Boston: Christian Science Publishing Society, 1991, p. 38.

42 Ibid.

43 Peel, p. 94.

44 Ibid., p. 96.

45 It is unclear what kind of abuse Mary is speaking of in the letter to her brother George, whether it is physical or verbal. However, Mary's family did seem to think she would be better off without her son, both physically and emotionally. See Peel, p. 96.

46 Mary Baker Eddy, *Retrospection and Introspection*, Boston: The First Church of Christ, Scientist, 1920, p. 30.

47 Peel, p. 98.

48 Ibid., p. 99.

49 Ibid., p. 109.

50 Ibid., p. 110.

51 Ibid.

52 Eddy, *Retrospection and Introspection*, p. 20.

CHAPTER 5: The Cure

53 Martin Gardner, *The Healing Revelations of Mary Baker Eddy: The Rise and Fall of Christian Science*, Buffalo, NY: Prometheus Books, 1993, p. 32.

54 Robert Peel, *Mary Baker Eddy: The Years of Discovery*, New York: Holt Rinehart and Winston, 1977, p. 167.

55 Irving Tomlinson, *Twelve Years with Mary Baker Eddy*, Boston: The Christian Science Publishing Society, 1945, p. 31.

56 Louise A. Smith, *Mary Baker Eddy: Discoverer and Founder of Christian Science*, Boston: Christian Science Publishing Society, 1991, p. 52.

57 Ibid.

58 Peel, p. 170.

59 Smith, pp. 55–56.

60 Ibid., p. 56.

61 Peel, p. 204.

62 Ibid., pp. 204–210.

63 Smith, p. 56.

64 Peel, p. 267.

65 Ibid., p. 221.

66 Ibid., p. 205.

67 Ibid., p. 244.

68 Ibid., p. 248.

69 Ibid., p. 249.

70 Ibid., p. 252.

71 Ibid.

72 Smith, pp. 63–64.

CHAPTER 6: Holding the Cross

73 Mary Baker Eddy, *Retrospection and Introspection*, Boston: The First Church of Christ, Scientist, 1920, p. 25.

74 Ibid.

75 Louise A. Smith, *Mary Baker Eddy: Discoverer and Founder of Christian Science*, Boston: Christian Science Publishing Society, 1991, p. 71.

76 Ibid.

77 Ibid., p. 70.

78 Eddy, *Retrospection and Introspection*, p. 37.

79 Robert Peel, *Mary Baker Eddy: The Years of Trial*, New York: Holt, Rinehart and Winston, 1977, p. 3.

80 Ibid., p. 5.

81 Smith, p. 73.

82 Peel, p. 21.

83 Ibid., p. 26.

84 Ibid., p. 28.

85 Ibid., p. 51.

86 Ibid., p. 58.

CHAPTER 7: Strengthening the Christian Science Movement

87 Robert Peel, *Mary Baker Eddy: The Years of Trial*, New York: Holt, Rinehart and Winston, 1977, p. 61.

88 Ibid., p. 83

89 Ibid.

90 Ibid., p. 86.

91 Ibid.

92 Ibid., p. 87.

93 Mary Baker Eddy, *Retrospection and Introspection*, Boston: The First Church of Christ, Scientist, 1920, p. 76.

94 Peel, p. 87.

95 Ibid.

96 Ibid., pp. 95–96.

97 Ibid., p. 97.

98 Ibid., pp. 97–98.

99 Ibid., p. 98.

100 Ibid., p. 117.

101 Ibid, p. 121.

102 Ibid., p. 123.

103 Louise A. Smith, *Mary Baker Eddy: Discoverer and Founder of Christian Science*, Boston: Christian Science Publishing Society, 1991, p. 83.

104 Ibid., p. 89.

CHAPTER 8: Starting Again

105 Robert Peel, *Mary Baker Eddy: The Years of Trial*, New York: Holt, Rinehart and Winston, 1977, p. 272.

106 Ibid.

107 Ibid., pp. 253–254.

108 Louise A. Smith, *Mary Baker Eddy: Discoverer and Founder of Christian Science*, Boston: Christian Science Publishing Society, 1991, p. 93.

109 Ibid., p. 95.
110 Irving Tomlinson, *Twelve Years with Mary Baker Eddy*, Boston: The Christian Science Publishing Society, 1945, p. 156.
111 Ibid.
112 Ibid., p. 157.
113 Smith, p. 96.
114 Ibid., p. 97.
115 Robert Peel, *Mary Baker Eddy: The Years of Authority*, New York: Holt, Rinehart and Winston, 1977, p. 68.
116 Ibid.
117 Ibid., p. 71.

CHAPTER 9:
Life at Pleasant View

118 Gillian Gill, *Mary Baker Eddy*, Cambridge, MA: Perseus Books, 1999, p. 399.
119 Ibid., p. 400.
120 Ibid., p. 413.
121 Ibid., p. 414.
122 Ibid., p. 421.
123 Robert Peel, *Mary Baker Eddy: The Years of Authority*, New York: Holt, Rinehart and Winston, 1977, p. 148.
124 Ibid., p. 155.
125 Ibid.
126 Gill, pp. 434–435.
127 Ibid., pp. 440–441.
128 Ibid., p. 442.
129 Ibid., p. 443.
130 Ibid., p. 445.
131 Peel, p. 173.

CHAPTER 10: The Final Years

132 Gillian Gill, *Mary Baker Eddy*, Cambridge, MA: Perseus Books, 1999, p. 473.
133 Ibid., p. 474.
134 Interview account is taken from Louise A. Smith, *Mary Baker Eddy: Discoverer and Founder of Christian Science*, Boston: Christian Science Publishing Society, 1991, p. 121.
135 Gill, p. 480.
136 Ibid., p. 486.
137 Ibid., p. 497.
138 Ibid., p. 505.
139 Ibid., p. 511.
140 The quotes in this paragraph were taken from a letter Mary wrote to Judge Chamberlain on May 16, 1907, as recorded in Gill, p. 512.
141 Ibid., p. 520.
142 Ibid., p. 525.
143 Ibid., p. 526.
144 Ibid., p. 525.
145 Robert Peel, *Mary Baker Eddy: The Years of Authority*, New York: Holt, Rinehart and Winston, 1977, p. 299.
146 Ibid., p. 311.
147 Ibid., p. 310.
148 Ibid.
149 Smith, p. 129.
150 Gill, p. 547.
151 Peel, *Authority*, p. 360.
152 Ibid.

Beasley, Norman. *Mary Baker Eddy: A Biography.* Duell, Sloan and Pearce, 1963.

Cather, Willa, and Georgine Milmine. *The Life of Mary Baker Eddy and the History of Christian Science.* University of Nebraska Press, 1993.

Eddy, Mary Baker. *Mary Baker Eddy: Speaking for Herself.* The Mary Baker Eddy Collection, 2002.

———. *Retrospection and Introspection.* The First Church of Christ, Scientist, 1920.

Gardner, Martin. *The Healing Revelations of Mary Baker Eddy: The Rise and Fall of Christian Science.* Prometheus Books, 1993.

Gill, Gillian. *Mary Baker Eddy.* Perseus Books, 1999.

Peel, Robert. *Mary Baker Eddy: The Years of Authority.* Holt, Rinehart and Winston, 1977.

———. *Mary Baker Eddy: The Years of Discovery.* Holt, Rinehart and Winston, 1966.

———. *Mary Baker Eddy: The Years of Trial.* Holt, Rinehart and Winston, 1971.

Silberger, Julius Jr. *Mary Baker Eddy: An Interpretive Biography of the Founder of Christian Science.* Little, Brown and Company, 1980.

Smith, Louise A. *Mary Baker Eddy: Discoverer and Founder of Christian Science.* Christian Science Publishing Society, 1991.

Thomas, Robert David. *With Bleeding Footsteps: Mary Baker Eddy's Path to Religious Leadership.* Alfred A. Knopf, 1994.

Tomlinson, Irving. *Twelve Years With Mary Baker Eddy.* The Christian Science Publishing Society, 1945.

Wilbur, Sibyl. *The Life of Mary Baker Eddy.* Concord Publishing Company, 1908.

FURTHER READING

PRIMARY SOURCES

Eddy, Mary Baker. *Letters of Mary Baker Eddy to Augusta E. Stetson, C.S.D.*, ed. Gail M. Weatherbe. Emma Publishing Society, 1990.

———. *Mary Baker Eddy: Speaking for Herself.* The Mary Baker Eddy Collection, 2002.

———. *Retrospection and Introspection.* The First Church of Christ, Scientist, 1920.

———. *Science and Health with Key to the Scriptures.* The First Church of Christ, Scientist.

Tomlinson, Irving. *Twelve Years with Mary Baker Eddy.* The Christian Science Publishing Society, 1945.

SECONDARY SOURCES

Cather, Willa and Georgine Milmine. *The Life of Mary Baker Eddy and the History of Christian Science.* University of Nebraska Press, 1993.

Gardner, Martin. *The Healing Revelations of Mary Baker Eddy: The Rise and Fall of Christian Science.* Prometheus Books, 1993.

Gill, Gillian. *Mary Baker Eddy.* Perseus Books, 1999.

Peel, Robert. *Mary Baker Eddy: The Years of Authority.* Holt Rinehart and Winston, 1977.

———. *Mary Baker Eddy: The Years of Discovery.* Holt Rinehart and Winston, 1966.

———. *Mary Baker Eddy: The Years of Trial.* Holt Rinehart and Winston, 1971.

Smith, Louise A. *Mary Baker Eddy: Discoverer and Founder of Christian Science.* Christian Science Publishing Society, 1991.

Thomas, Robert David. *With Bleeding Footsteps: Mary Baker Eddy's Path to Religious Leadership.* Alfred A. Knopf, 1994.

WEBSITES

Church of Christ, Scientist

http://www.tfccs.com/index.jhtml;jsessionid=HIH3UQ4SCDT1VKGL4L2SFEQ

Official site of the Church of Christ, Scientist; includes historical and biographical information on Eddy and the Church, as well as information about Christian Science publications and activities.

Healing Unlimited

http://www.christianscience.org/HUIntro.htm

Includes detailed information about the theology of Christian Science, with pages devoted to Church publications, activities, and news.

The Mary Baker Eddy Institute

http://www.mbeinstitute.org/

Site devoted to providing information about Eddy to educate the public and promote Christian Science ideals.

The Mary Baker Eddy Library for the Betterment of Humanity

http://www.marybakereddylibrary.org/

Includes extensive information on principles of Christian Science as well as photographs and documents from the life of Mary Baker Eddy.

INDEX

INDEX

ABOUT THE CONTRIBUTORS

RACHEL A. KOESTLER-GRACK has worked with nonfiction books as an editor and writer since 1999. She lives on a hobby farm near Glencoe, Minnesota. During her career, she has worked extensively with historical topics, including the colonial era, the Civil War era, the Great Depression, and the civil rights movement.

MARTIN E. MARTY is an ordained minister in the Evangelical Lutheran Church and the Fairfax M. Cone Distinguished Service Professor Emeritus at the University of Chicago Divinity School, where he taught for thirty-five years. Marty has served as president of the American Academy of Religion, the American Society of Church History, and the American Catholic Historical Association, and was also a member of two U.S. presidential commissions. He is currently Senior Regent at St. Olaf College in Northfield, Minnesota. Marty has written more than fifty books, including the three-volume *Modern American Religion* (University of Chicago Press). His book *Righteous Empire* was a recipient of the National Book Award.